Gadgets and gurus,
I've tried them all
But they're never there
when I take a fall

Ayden, this book
May open your
mind & your
♡.
From my heart
to

From the VIP Section...

"*Gadgets and Gurus* is a masterful, visionary, heart-filled guide to joyful and abundant living. I am deeply moved by the depth of Jeff Tressler's sharing, and I know this book can change your life if you apply its vibrant principles."

– Alan Cohen, Best-selling author of the
The Dragon Doesn't Live Here Anymore

"*Gadgets and Gurus* is a wonderful book about finding your own soulful connection to life and all living things. Jeff's insightfully written poems, stories and perspectives will pierce your heart with visions of a world where we have a choice to be joyful, loving, compassionate and conscious."

–Michael Tomlinson, Singer/Songwriter

"I love to read. I love words and Jeff uses them so beautifully."

– Melinda Rappold, Winter Park, FL

"Reading is my favorite pastime. This book has great continuity and is very focused. It's also fun, inspiring and easy to read."

– Sany, Tampa, FL

"I came home and found the book on my dining room table. I just unplugged and started reading. Before long, I started thinking of the people I loved who I wanted to buy the book for."

– Alan Brady, Longwood, FL

Gadgets
&
Gurus

*A Lighter Look At
Enlightenment*

Gadgets & Gurus

A Lighter Look At Enlightenment

JEFF TRESSLER

Circle of Three Publishing
Orlando, Florida

Circle of Three Publishing
Copyright © 1999 by Jeff Tressler
All rights reserved.

Circle of Three Publishing
P.O. Box 533902, Orlando, Florida 32853-3902

Printed in Canada.

Cover design: Cathy Sanders

Back cover artwork: Mama Pearl Routon,
Mural in First Baptist Church, Paris, TN

All graphic illustrations are professional enhancements
of the author's original doodles.

ISBN 0-9672177-0-9

Think about it,
there must be a higher Love
Down in the Heart or
hidden in the stars above.
Without it, life is wasted time
Look inside your Heart,
I'll look inside mine.[1]

STEVE WINWOOD
"Higher Love"

Table Of Contents

Acknowledgements

Almost from the time I could talk, I was prolifically quoting the words of famous people. In the beginning, I was influenced by sports figures. By the time I was in my late teens, it became the great prophets of my time, Bob Dylan, Carol King, Eric Clapton and most especially Dan Fogelberg. For more than 25 years now, I have been spreading the gospel according to rock 'n roll.

Finally, after using other people's lines and giving them due credit for all these years, I began putting my own thoughts on paper. My poems and stories are a unique blend of my own language, and the influence of the lyrics and the lines of many different musicians and authors. Ultimately, however, these influences were a Divine gift.

It has been said that *life* is God's gift to *us* and what we *do* with it is our gift to *God*. This book is an expression of God's gift to me. I suppose then that the offering of its contents to the world is my gift to God and to you, another beautiful and unique aspect of the creator.

So many people have contributed to my growth and hence to this book that I can't possibly remember them all, let alone thank them all. But here are a few:

I want to thank Murriah McMaster for her spiritual guidance, for introducing me to Unity churches and the books of Florence Scoval Schinn.

Thank you to Unity Churches for introducing me to Christianity in a new and glorious way.

Linda, Dawn, Cat and Kim for their enthusiastic support and encouragement of this Divine project.

While I trace the foundation of my spiritual influence to the musical prophets, the author who most recently has inspired and reminded me that the music is inside of us all is Alan Cohen. Alan is a most masterful translator of messages from a pure human Heart.

Cathy Sanders for everything. As a gift to me, Cat created the poetry book which is what this book evolved from. She urged me to write the book and has worked tirelessly with the design, graphics, layout and typesetting. She was committed to making it beautiful and she succeeded.

Thanks to Cat's sister, Annie, Joe and Matt for special artistic contributions.

Gabriel H. Vaughan for his design help and counsel on all matters of the publishing process.

Becky Farmerie for fixing things up, putting commas, colons and all that other punctuation stuff in all the right places.

The Circle of Three for demonstrating the Power of Love to make this dream a reality.

Ultimately, without the high standards of truth, fairness and equality, upheld and instilled in me by my mother, Eileen Tressler, I never would have gotten this far.

With deepest Love and
gratitude to all.

Introduction

Gadgets And Gurus: A Lighter Look At Enlightenment is a by-product of a collection of my of original poetry entitled "Songs of the Spirit." *Gadget And Gurus* includes poems from that collection, poems of spiritual Love and life, the stories behind the poems, their inspiration and complementary tales of other life experiences with applicable references to other authors, songwriters and storytellers who have influenced me along the way. By their very nature, these are the stories of *all* our lives in some way.

The essence of these poems and stories is not new. However, I hope that they are presented in a fresh and unique way that will capture the reader's attention and send a message straight to the intended target, the Heart.

It is inside our Hearts that we will find the most sought after answers to our most pressing questions. Finding the key to open our Hearts has not been an easy task for most people. Thus the answers to our questions about life have eluded the vast majority of us.

There is a well known story about God that goes something like this: God is looking for a safe hiding place for the secrets of life, a place where no one would look. After considering the highest mountain and the deepest ocean, God decided that man would always find his secrets there, so he hid them in the place where humans would be the most unlikely to look, inside of them.

Hopefully this book will help you to look to the only place where you can truly find your answers, *inside.* Even though God hid the answers there, if you go there you will find Him.

I don't think of God as having gender, but for simplicity's sake I use the masculine pronoun. I also have come to use *God, Love* and *The Universe* interchangeably. You will see all three references used in different places with the same meaning. I most commonly use Love because it is non-divisive. In some sense everyone believes in Love, not everyone believes in God.

The basic premise of my belief system is that Love is the most powerful force in the world and is at the core of all true healing; i.e., no matter what vehicle is used, the essence of all true healing is Love.

So this book is dedicated to healing our own Hearts, our own families, our communities and our world. We live in a world that is full of things, things to entertain us, things to drive, and many things to show off, yet millions of people still feel empty. The world is crying out to be healed. The world is crying out for Love. Everything we need is already there on the inside and it's time to help each other find it. In so doing, we will build bridges that will unite and heal us all, Heart to Heart.

> *It's all on the inside, to say you could find*
> *It elsewhere would be wrong.*
> *It's all on the inside, each soul has its song.*[1]

MICHAEL FRANKS
"It's All On The Inside"

℘

Special Dedication

To the memory of two of the purest
Hearts to grace the planet in the 20th century.

Mother Teresa,
the Mother of all Hearts everywhere
and
Diana, Princess of Wales,
the Queen of Hearts.

While your spirits soar doing
your great work in other ways,
may your voices live on in our Hearts.

Love is the answer,
That's really the way
When you're feeling lowly,
Give some away

Gadgets And Gurus

We are in an age of spiritual awakening. That is certainly a good reason to celebrate, but to think that we've arrived is incredibly naive. There seems to be a polarization taking place right now. On one hand there are larger and larger numbers of people who are coming together to join in raising their spiritual consciousness. At the same time the headlines are filled like never before with stories of drive-by shootings and mass murders. One week the cover of *Time* magazine is graced by the image of an Angel, the next week a terrorist. The fight of the century features a man wearing shorts with the inscription "It is the Christ within that strengthens me" against a man cussing and mocking God.

Yes, we are waking up but we have just begun. Caroline Myss, author of the audio series *Energy Anatomy*,[1] notes that about two decades ago there was a critical mass shift in consciousness. It yielded a pronouncement that we could heal ourselves simply by changing our thoughts. In spite of this new awareness, Myss states that such a healing is still rare enough that it makes big news when it happens, when it should be so commonplace that it receives little mention.

Launch Delay

In September of 1993, I made a spontaneous decision to take a trip to Unity Village. Unity Village is the headquarters for Unity churches, located just outside of Kansas City, Missouri. For those who align themselves with teachings of Unity, going to Unity Village is equivalent to a person of the Muslim faith going to Mecca.

One fine fall day my spiritual sister Linda and I set off on a cross country road trip from Orlando to Kansas City. We were equipped with all essentials including the most important item of all, musical cassette tapes. We had many tapes that you could pick up at any record store, but the most special tape of all was a homemade blend of melodies by our favorite artists, ranging from Dan Fogelberg to Santana. There were also many others whose music was evolving much like we were, in a very spiritual manner. We titled this tape "Songs For The Spirit." The music was more than just listening material. It was our companion and our lead for singing and dancing. It was designed to move our spirit and that's exactly what it did for us.

Between tapes we would talk about lots of wonderful things. Our favorite topic was the growing spiritual movement, not only in America, but throughout the world. I told Linda that there was a time in my life that if I opened my mouth and talked spirit, I was usually speaking a language that people didn't understand. By this time in September of 1993, it was a language that people seemed to be speaking on every street corner. I no longer felt like I was a foreigner in my own land.

The experience at Unity Village enhanced my feelings ten fold. We made many friends and had many Divine experiences. It seemed that this retreat was a gathering place for us to share our inspiration, reinforce our beliefs and grow on many dimensions. I was sure that we were all disciples who would cast our seeds of goodness and Love and be witness to the fields growing white for the harvest. The planet was awakening.

To erase any doubt about these feelings, I received a sure sign as a gift from a new friend. The gift was a book called the *Celestine Prophecy.* The book is said to be fiction. However, to me, the book was a profound depiction of the consciousness that the human race was rapidly moving into. It seemed that this expansion of spiritual consciousness was moving so fast that soon we would all be ascended beings of light.

I went home from that trip full of hope. I began to make plans to change many things in my life. I was sure that my days of suffering were over. I was

Soon we would all be ascended beings of light.

wrong. With all that was going on, all of the books, all the gatherings, all the workshops, I was still struggling in many areas of my life. When I looked around I realized that I had a lot of company. The scariest part was that I recognized the faces. Many of them were the disciples who I had expected to join me in the ascension. Instead they had joined me in the plunge. What happened? Why was our launch delayed?

> *I look around for the friends that*
> *I used to turn to pull me through*
> *Looking into their eyes*
> *I see them running too.[2]*

> JACKSON BROWNE
> "Running On Empty"

> ✿

Who's Primitive?

I think our problem is that most of us are just too darn busy. Busyness is the most prevalent and dangerous disease in the United States of America. Being spiritual does not make you immune. Many of the most dedicated truth seekers are obviously worn out from trying to keep up.

Mass numbers of them are spending all of their time and money going to workshops to figure out how to save time and money. Each time they go out with the hope that this time, at this workshop, they will be given the magic formula. But there's always another workshop and always the same tired look in their eyes. That's a very familiar look, I've seen it many times in my own mirror.

I have benefited greatly from many wonderful workshops and many wonderful speakers, However, in my experience, the greatest workshop of all is everyday life. I believe that you will find this to be true if you go out into the world holding only two of the principles of Attitudinal Healing in your mind. These principles are: *We are students and teachers to each other* (Principle #9) and *We can become Love finders rather that fault finders* (Principle #7). Practice these principles and you will indeed find that everyday life is the greatest classroom of all.

An important exercise in this classroom is to be willing to look deeply into people eyes. The movie *Nell* is a compelling story of a young women who is raised primitively on a lake in the Appalachian mountains, miles away from civilization. She had been living alone there in a cabin with her elderly mother when she was discovered. There was no record of her birth. She had been born out of wedlock and her mother wanted to keep it a secret. When a grocery delivery boy found her mother lying dead on the floor of their remote cabin, Nell was soon to be discovered by the outside world. The old lady died of natural causes leaving behind a "wild child," a being unlike anything city folks had ever seen. Nell

We are all students and teachers to each other.

Attitudinal Healing Principle #9

became the object of scientific studies and petty legal battles. Ultimately, she would end up in a courtroom where it would be decided where she would live and who would take care of her.

During the trial Nell carefully studied the courtroom proceedings. As the trial neared its conclusion she asked to speak to the court in her own primitive language as translated by her researcher-turned-friend, Jerry. This is what she said, "Since my mother died I've been alone. I've been afraid. Everyone's frightened, everywhere. The sweet Lord soothes our tears, our many tears. You have big things. You know big things, but you don't look into each other's eyes and you are hungry for quietness. I have lived a small life, I know small things...Don't be frightened for Nell. Don't weep for her, I have no greater sorrows than you."[3]

For Nell (played by Jodie Foster), a small life meant a slow, quiet and simple life and a big life is a fast, loud and complicated one. The small things she referred to included innocence, how to know a person and feel a person just by looking into their eyes. She understood that we could touch each other's soul that way and that it could heal and unite us. She also knew that we desperately needed peace and that the place to find that peace was in quietness.

Life In The Fast Lane

This title is not new but it cannot be overused. Most people don't realize how much it applies to them or have gotten so caught up in it that they can't see the forrest for the trees.

When people aren't attending workshops to figure out how to save time and money they're looking in the fast lane for other angles. Faster cars, faster computers, faster foods, faster communications. The grand irony here is that the faster our gadgets get the more worn out we become. The computer age was once a promise to free up our time. Instead it has become a monster that is swallowing it up. It seems that our lives are emulating our technology. We keep moving at a faster pace to keep up with the machines that were supposed to be our saviors.

How do we unplug ourselves from this enslavement to the gadgets and gurus? Do we smash our computers and fire our therapists? That's a little too extreme. I wouldn't recommend anyone going that far. We can, however, change our priorities, slow down and become human beings again instead of human doings. Then we'll be able to look into each other's eyes, make a connection and gently remind each other of our true nature.

You have big things. You know big things, but you don't look into each other's eyes and you are hungry for quietness.

The movie "Nell"

When Duty Calls
Ignore It

This is a "handle with care" suggestion until you realize its true meaning.

The Buddha said that there are three impediments to enlightenment: *lust, fear and duty.*

Most people get the first two, lust and fear, right off. For the third, most people are likely to say greed, not duty. I think the reason that there aren't four impediments is because greed and lust are essentially the same thing.

Why duty? Because duty implies that the only reason we are doing something is because we feel obligated. We're not doing it because we Love doing it or because it will help us grow, we are doing it simply because it's our duty. When our behavior is motivated by duty we actually stop living for the period of time we have devoted to that particular duty. The best lesson that we can learn is that in every moment there is an opportunity to practice mindfulness. Then you'll know that in every moment there is a gift, if we'll just wake up enough to notice it when it appears.

In the movie *Dead Poet's Society,* the unconventional literature teacher Mr. Keating is passionate about teaching his students about "Carpe Diem," the Latin term for "seize the day." In one impassioned talk he huddled his students around him and said, "Boys, listen up. We don't read and write poetry because it's cute. We read and write poetry because we are members of the human race, and the human race is filled with passion. Medicine, Law, Business and Engineering are all noble pursuits and necessary to sustain life, but beauty, poetry, romance, Love, these are what we stay alive for."[4]

The Little Pieces

If Love is what we stay alive for, perhaps our healing dilemma won't be solved until we realize we are all suffering from not enough Love. For us to heal, we must realize that we are made of the same things. Then we can begin to work in partnership with each other, with the planet, with God.

In the movie *Phenomenon*, John Travolta played the character of George, an individual who became a genius virtually overnight. One night he used his mind to break a top secret government Morse code, just for fun. When the "Fed's" finally caught up to him, not realizing that his intentions were innocent, they arrested him and put him through a battery of tests, to measure his intelligence. After a long, and for him, boring, series of tests George began to move a pencil back and forth without actually touching it with his hand. He was using something commonly known as telekinesis. His stunned researcher asked him how he was doing that. George answered by saying, "Well, I could say that I am willing it to move but that wouldn't be quite accurate. Actually it's more like a partnership. You know we're all made out of the same stuff, Bob." Bob, the researcher, looks up incredulously

Beauty,

poetry,

romance,

Love,

these are

what

we stay

alive for.

The movie
"Dead Poet's
Society"

and questions, wood? Travolta says "Energy, Bob, you know, the little pieces."[5]

Nature And Nurture

The place where we most realize our connected-ness is when we are with our common mother, Mother Nature. She will always nurture us even when it is unavailable elsewhere. When looking for Love, Mother Nature is a reliable source. When you Love her back it will open up new dimensions to Love.

Far more than the worship of any guru, religion or technology we need to learn the art of Love. We need to bring passion into our lives every day by Loving our children, our parents, our grocery store clerk. We need to speak to each other from our Hearts, smile at each other with the brilliance of the sun, and touch each other with the tenderness of a flower petal. If we do these things one day we'll look up and realize that God is standing right there beside us.

Gadgets And Gurus

Gadgets and gurus, that's where to look
If I don't find it there, I'll get another book
One that will show me the way out of this mess
Yeah that's a good way, maybe that's best
If that doesn't do it, I'll buy myself a tape
That will pump me all up and make me feel great
If that doesn't do it, I'll take myself a class
If all else should fail that will save me at last

Play like a child and learn how to fly
Don't be absurd, I won't even try
Well of course birds fly they have wings that I don't
I'm playing it safe, no leaping for me, I simply won't
I won't and I can't; Something's holding me back
Those authors and gurus; They know the way
They'll tell me how if I'll just listen to what they say

Gadgets and gurus, I've tried them all
But they're never there when I take a fall

Love is the answer, that's really the way
When you're feeling lowly, give some away
When Love comes to you don't close the door
Open up and receive it then give out some more
Let it flow out of you then back in again
That is the secret, I tell you my friend;
Open your Heart and feel how it feels
It's what life is about, it's really what's real

So the answer to your prayers
comes on the wings of a Dove
Singing remember three things: Love, Love, and Love

WILLOW BEND, FLORIDA, SUMMER 1997

Pose it to your heart
and the answer will come,
not just for the chosen,
not just for some

The Melody Of Life

On April 30, 1985, Eileen Tressler, the most Loving and generous person I've ever known, who just happened to be my mother, passed away. It took me 25 years to realize how wonderful she really was and by the time I was 30 she was gone. At that time, and for many years to come, it seemed that the only real Love, the unconditional Love of a Mother, was gone forever. Finally, in the fall of 1992, I came to know Love again as I was adopted by a new mother, Mother Earth.

I had spent most of the years in between working very hard to create a niche for myself professionally. After a considerable struggle I had managed to put myself in a position where I was financially comfortable, in a high profile corporate position in an impressive office with a view. In spite of it all, I was miserable.

The turning point for me came when I was introduced to a new album and a new song. For a song to have an influence on my life is not an unusual occurrence. As I've mentioned before my greatest prophets have been the purveyors of rock 'n roll, but this song had a more profound and lasting impact than any before. The album was Kenny Loggins' *Leap of Faith* and the song was "Conviction of the Heart." The song is passionate with a deep and beautiful message, and a call to awaken to the need to Love our planet with conviction.

Starting in September of 1992, and for many months thereafter, I would begin every day listening to, and dancing with the song. I'd keep playing it until I had my walking clothes on, and when I was dressed I would hit the door singing "One with the Earth, with the sky, One with everything in life,"[1] the song's chorus. This became my mantra every morning as I breathed in the fresh air around Orlando's Lake Ivanhoe and cruised its shoreline, communing with the Lake, the Sky, the Earth and all of the creatures in all of those elements.

When I would finish the exercise portion of the walk, I would go down to the water's edge and, for the first time in my life, I became interested in birds. I would spend as much time as I could getting lost in the flight patterns of the birds, the primary residents of the lake.

There were all kinds of birds at Lake Ivanhoe, big birds, little birds, colorful birds and not so colorful birds. As I witnessed them in flight, I noticed that some flew with seemingly effortless ease, and others, especially the little birds, looked like they were having to flap their wings really hard to stay in the air. It seemed to me then that they had much more in common with people than I had previously realized.

There was a lot going on inside of me at the

same time that all these splendid events were going on outside of me. My Heart was opening, I was falling in Love. I was falling in Love with the music–the music playing from the stereo, from the lake and from inside of me. I was falling in Love with life. I was realizing my oneness with it all as I repeated this mantra over and over again in my mind. I was beginning to feel Love and self acceptance and I was beginning to dream. I began to dream about learning to fly, symbolically speaking.

> *One with the Earth, with the sky,*
> *One with everything in life*
> *I believe it will start*
> *with conviction of the Heart.*[1]
>
> KENNY LOGGINS & GUY LINDER
> "Conviction Of The Heart"

℘

I was adopted by a new mother, Mother Earth.

Whose Dream Is It, Anyway?

In the movie *Field of Dreams*, Ray, the character played by Kevin Costner, began to build a baseball field in the middle of nowhere, his own cornfield in Iowa. He started building it because he had a dream in which he heard a voice say, "if you build it he will come," and had a vision of a baseball field. Though it wasn't clear to him at the time why he was to build the field, he discovered that he was creating a space for the spirits of great baseball players to come back and play baseball again on the Earth plane. It also allowed him to heal a relationship with someone who had dreamed of being a great baseball player but didn't quite make it, his deceased father.

Whether it's a voice, a vision, or just a feeling, we all get messages about fulfilling our dreams. But most of us just dismiss them and go about our daily routines following someone else's plans for us. What we are doing is what Wayne Dyer refers to as fulfilling our "Tribal" responsibilities. If you are a citizen of the United States of America, that is your tribe, and you are probably haunted by an implanted belief in something called the American Work Ethic. According to this ethic, if you work very hard in an accepted tribal occupation then you can have what every tribal member wants, a big car, a big house, and other symbols of tribal success. If you don't have those aspirations, if a normal job is not your desire and the most important things to you aren't the big car and the big house, the tribe is likely to disapprove and you will not be accepted by them.

The grand paradox here is that people have convinced themselves that they are doing what they are doing so they can acquire those things that the tribe has convinced them that they want. In reality, it's the tribe that says they want these things when what they really want the most is to be accepted by the tribe.

Acceptance equals Love and Love's what we all really want. The difficulty here is to silence the haunting voice of the tribe so that we can hear our own voice. If it still says that you want the things the tribe wants and under their unspoken conditions, then you're on your way. If what you want is something different, you have to be brave enough to follow your own voice at the risk of losing the tribe's acceptance. In the final analysis, you have to trust and accept yourself, and trust in God or you will end up living someone else's dream.

> One road was simple,
> Acceptance of life,
> The other road offered sweet peace,
> When I made my decision
> My vision became my release.[2]

DAN FOGELBERG
"Netherlands"

℘

Acceptance equals Love and Love's what we all really want.

Recapturing Your Dreams

I mentioned that I had begun to dream again in the fall of 1992. Watching birds in flight gave me a symbolic message about how we had been conditioned to believe in our limitations. I also came to believe that it was God's intention for us to soar. This was not the first time that I'd had dreams, but this time I was operating under faith that they would be fulfilled. Now, I was willing to go the distance by taking things one step at a time, allowing them to happen according to God's timetable, not mine.

To quote Peter Carlson, an Orlando area counselor, teacher of Mindfulness Meditation, and a Professional Human Being, "we live in a plop-plop, fizz-fizz society." We want to take a pill and instantly get better and we want our dreams to manifest overnight. It took me many years to understand Jesus' Biblical message, "Do not be anxious about your life," but in my Heart I know it now and realize that our most worthwhile dreams often take years to manifest.

One piece of my dream came together in a rather small but wonderful way. It was January 1994, and I had been attending Unity Church of Christianity in Orlando, Florida (I have made my home in the Orlando area most of my life) for about a year. One Sunday our new minister gave a sermon on reclaiming your dreams. During the talk I heard the lyrics to "Conviction of the Heart" playing in my mind, these lyrics, "Where are the dreams that we once had, this is the time to bring them back."[3] So, I approached the minister, Bob Marshall, and "witnessed" to him about this song that had such a profound affect on my life and asked him if we could fit it into the service some time. Bob referred me to Jamie, the music director. While waiting to speak to Jamie, I discussed the matter with Jamie's girlfriend, Suzie, who suggested that we have a '60s party, dress up in hippie clothes and listen to the music of the era. We immediately spoke to Bob who had a much larger vision and suggested that we have a full blown retreat with music, meditation and much more. Within 45 minutes of the time that I first mentioned the song, we had formed a committee to plan the first Unity Church of Christianity retreat, with a '60s theme to boot.

The reason the '60s theme came into focus was related to my interpretation of the lyrics, "Where are the dreams that we once had, this is the time to bring them back." The way that I understood this was that we baby boomers had the right idea, the right dreams back in the '60s. It was then that there was a mass movement in consciousness about real values, peace and Love, brotherhood and sisterhood, truth and compassion. That also was the time when the ecological movement was born.

Our most worthwhile dreams often take years to manifest.

So the retreat was on and through some arm twisting on my part, it was named *Recapturing Our Dreams, A Vision Quest.* We would start on Friday night and offer people the option to stay at the church overnight or go home and return on Saturday morning for a full day of spiritual merriment. We planned the retreat for 50 people and 100 showed up.

I was delighted to be the music director for this event. I felt that music was the seed from which the whole thing sprouted and the energy which would hold it all together.

After our registration on Friday night, we would sing Beatles songs to kick things off and sing them as often as the good Reverend would allow us to.

The retreat was a tremendous success. We sang, we were guided in meditation, we were guided in spiritual dances. We gathered in one large group and broke up in small groups identified by a selected Beatles tune. My group was "A Hard Days Night," a huge misnomer for this affair. As we wrapped things up we gathered in our small groups and each person drew their own picture of the world of their dreams. The form and talent of each picture was unique, but as you might imagine, the themes of Love, peace and harmony were a common thread that weaved them all together. Here is a journal note of mine from that evening:

> *Never in my life have I experienced anything like this before. One hundred people all Loving each other unconditionally. Joy, Love and happiness on every face. Unsurpassed energy from the collective consciousness carrying everyone to ever higher heights. Sharing, caring and opening up the Heart. Like Rev. Bob said, by Saturday everyone knew that everyone there was a "beautiful child of God."*

For the next week after the retreat all the people I talked to had the same curious response, "I feel like I'm in Love."

We paved the way at this first retreat for many more wonderful retreats. The retreats have become

```
          LOVE                      LOVE
      LOVE  LOVE  LOVE          LOVE  LOVE  LOVE
    LOVE  LOVE  LOVE  LOVE    LOVE  LOVE  LOVE  LOVE
  LOVE  LOVE  LOVE  LOVE  LOVE  LOVE  LOVE  LOVE  LOVE
LOVE LOVE LOVE LOVE LOVE LOVE LOVE LOVE LOVE LOVE LOVE
LOVE LOVE LOVE LOVE LOVE LOVE LOVE LOVE LOVE LOVE LOVE
LOVE LOVE LOVE LOVE LOVE LOVE LOVE LOVE LOVE LOVE LOVE
LOVE LOVE LOVE LOVE LOVE LOVE LOVE LOVE LOVE LOVE LOVE
  LOVE LOVE LOVE LOVE LOVE LOVE LOVE LOVE LOVE LOVE
  LOVE LOVE LOVE LOVE LOVE LOVE LOVE LOVE LOVE LOVE
    LOVE LOVE LOVE LOVE LOVE LOVE LOVE LOVE LOVE
      LOVE LOVE LOVE LOVE LOVE LOVE LOVE LOVE
      LOVE LOVE LOVE LOVE LOVE LOVE LOVE
        LOVE LOVE LOVE LOVE LOVE LOVE
        LOVE LOVE LOVE LOVE LOVE
          L O V E L O V E L O V E
          L O V E L O V E L O V E
            L O V E L O V E
              L  O  V  E
              L O V E
```

famous and draw people from miles around, many who don't normally attend the church.

What this retreat represented, among other things, were the possibilities that exist if we can produce the right environment, born out of the right intention. When we do, we incubate a Heaven on Earth, a place where we can all live harmoniously. We conducted the experiment, we succeeded and now it is scientifically proven.

Keep a Heart full of Love and a mind full of joy, then no other tasks will you need to employ.

Heart Full Of Love

Sober This Time

Everywhere you look there is evidence of a spiritual awakening right here on planet Earth. There is evidence everywhere of the "New Age." I'm not sure when this new age was supposed to have begun but I would suggest to you that in many ways it began in the United States, at least, in the 1960s. During the '60s there were thousands of flower children who were running around displaying peace symbols and singing songs about brotherhood. A new language was formed using words like cool and groovy, and talk about good and bad vibes. War was bad, peace was good. Hatred was bad, Love was good. Racism was bad, acceptance of everyone was good. Materialism was bad, non-materialism was good.

This last quality was misunderstood and was probably the undoing of the movement, temporarily. Eventually, reality set in and the flower children discovered that there were bills to pay and traded in their faded jeans for business suits.

For some who have recently joined the current spiritual movement this stuff is all new to them. For others it is quite familiar. These are the dreams that we once had, the ones that Kenny Loggins sings about–the dreams that we had in the renaissance period of the '60s. Yes, it's bigger now, encompassing an even more diverse population of people and you don't have to smoke pot to under-

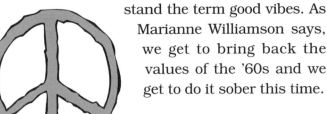

stand the term good vibes. As Marianne Williamson says, we get to bring back the values of the '60s and we get to do it sober this time.

Where Have You Been?

So where did the consciousness that was raised in the '60s go for three decades? Why the apparent disappearing act?

Perhaps the same thing happened to the collective consciousness in the '60s that happens to every truth seeker in their quest for enlightenment. According to a general consensus from almost all truth teachings and from personal experience, to gain enlightenment you must let go of the ego. This is perhaps the greatest challenge you'll ever encounter. The ego doesn't want to die and it will protect itself by throwing everything unlike Love, peace and joy in the way of your path to enlightenment.

In the '60s, masses of people were coming together to spread the message of Love, peace and joy. They were beginning the process of detaching from the ego.

Suppose, if you will, that the '70s represented a time in which the ego rebelled and things continued to get uglier right into the '80s.

Perhaps it's no coincidence that the '80s represented one of the most profound periods of materialism in the history of this country. Money was easy to make and many were exploiting legal ways of stealing to fatten their

If you could just Love enough you would be the happiest and most powerful person in the world.

Emmit Fox

wallets and purses. America was worshipping the golden calf like never before. Then the Savings and Loans collapsed and many good paying jobs disappeared. That's the bad news.

The good news is that the consciousness that was raised in the '60s never died. It was just lying dormant waiting for the right time to erupt. When the materialism of the '80s left us empty, we had something wonderful to fall back on, God. The dreamers from the '60s are now being joined by a whole new generation who are seeking and promoting a life and a world where Love, peace, and joy are the prevailing principles.

The key for this new generation is to stay focused on matters of the Heart and to dream these dreams individually, collectively and most importantly, consciously.

Pull The Cork

Everyone is familiar with the story of the Genie. The Genie has the power to grant you any wish (or wishes) that your Heart desires. First you must find the Genie, who according to folklore, usually resides in a bottle or a lamp. Your job is to free the Genie and if you do, your reward is that you get to make a wish and have it granted.

People rarely find the Genie, and anyone who does is considered to be very lucky. Often that lucky individual makes wishes that don't make them happy. The story of the Genie is our story. It is the story of every human being.

It is our story, first of all because of our belief system. We believe that having our wishes granted,

our dreams fulfilled and assuring ourselves of happiness is as rare as the
Genie.

Another reason it's our story is
because we all have those opportunities in life to make a wish and when we
get our wish we discover that it doesn't
make us happy. Those wishes are often
disguised as choices. The job we
choose, the mate we select and the car
we drive usually began as a wish.

The truth is the Genie lives within
us all. Inside each person resides a
powerful and creative being who has
the magic to make all our dreams come
true. This Genie knows all of our
thoughts and dreams but cannot distinguish between the good ones and
the bad ones so that those occurrences
that look like bad luck are actually our
dreams coming true.

Since our thoughts have creative
power, it is our challenge to create consciously. For most of our lives we have
been creating unconsciously, partially
because we didn't understand how
powerful negative thoughts could be
and partially because we made choices
that were in accordance with a standard created by our society, not our
Heart.

Listen to your thoughts. Then listen
to your Heart. Make a conscious effort
to make the two match. Hear what the

Inside each person resides a powerful and creative being who has the magic to make all our dreams come true.

Genie is hearing. Then pull the cork and set it free. Once you have, tell it what you really want, you know, the things your Heart told you it wanted.

> *People can you feel it,*
> *Love is everywhere*
> *People can you hear it,*
> *A song is in the air.*[4]

> DICKEY BETTS
> "Revival"

The Melody Of Life

It was a good day for turtles
And fishes galore
Big fishes, little fishes
And oh so much more

There were birds that were winging
And others were singing
It became clear to me then
That the Heavens were ringing
With the melody of life
You could see, feel and hear
I just tuned into the channel
And let Angels draw near

What channel's it on
Where do I find it on the dial
You may be asking yourself
With a most bewildered smile

Pose it to your Heart
And the answer will come
Not just for the chosen
Not just for some
See, we're all really Angels
Each and every one

So tune into the channel
Your Heart knows the way
And feel the sweet melody of life
Every breath, every moment, every single day

CRANES ROOST PARK, ALTAMONTE SPRINGS, FLORIDA, WINTER 1997

*Keep a heart full of love and
a mind full of joy then
no other tasks will you need to employ*

Heart Full Of Love

During one of those magical walks around the lake, prior to the time that I wrote the poem "Heart Full Of Love," I had a notion about the emptiness that I had felt most of my life and a vision came to mind. The vision was that of a box. The box had a label on it that said "Love." The box was always empty and I kept trying to fill it. Like so many others, I would put things in it like alcohol, drugs and other toxic substances. Sometimes, just for a little while it would seem like the box would fill up. Yet every time that I'd go to bed thinking that I had filled the box, I'd wake up the next morning only to find it empty again.

It's my belief that every aberrant behavior is just an attempt to fill that box. Everything that we take on as a result of it is just a substitute for Love.

What has changed, for the most part for me, is that I have learned not to look outside of myself to fill the need for Love but to look within. Inside there is a wellspring of Love that is actually crying to be let out and as soon as I extend myself with an open Heart

I draw Love back into me. This spiritual law works for everyone but it doesn't fit into the accounting system that we have been conditioned to believe in by our society. According to the American Social Accounting System (ASAS), if a man gives a women roses, for instance, she owes him affection. The ASAS system has nothing at all to do with Love. Real Love is something you freely share without the condition that you will get something in return. The paradox here is that if you give something in the spirit of Love you will always get a return on your investment. However, it may not come from the person to whom it was given.

> *We are all born for Love.*
> *It is the principle of existence*
> *And its only end.*
>
> BENJAMIN DISRAELI

༄

Reduce It For Expansion

The movie *Michael* was about a most unusual angel (Michael) who was played by John Travolta. He was a big man with large wings, an angel in human form. A group of reporters from a tabloid newspaper discovered Michael and were going to unveil this living angel in their scandal column. Michael agreed to go with them from the Milk Bottle Motel in rural Iowa back to Chicago under one condition. They would have to make the trip in his favorite car, an old beat up station wagon.

All the while that they were driving, Michael sat in the back of the station wagon drinking beer and smoking cigarettes. He was always joyful and, during one scene, he leaned forward and asked his three reporter/traveling companions if they knew what the key was to reaching Heaven. No, they all replied. He gave them a clue, "You remember what John and Paul said?" One reporter inquired, "the apostles?" Michael, "No, the Beatles, dummy. They said, all you need is Love. Join me in a chorus would you." They all started singing.

In this complex world it seems like too simple of an answer but that's the whole point. We've been conditioned to believe that it's hard, so it is. Reduce the equation to Love and watch your horizons expand.

Reduce the equation to Love and watch your horizons expand.

The Debilitating Blessing

For those who need scientific evidence of the importance that Love plays in our lives, Dr. Deepak Chopra gives a powerful illustration of it in his book *Ageless Body Timeless Mind*. He refers to a condition called psychosocial dwarfism, a syndrome that occurs in children who feel so unloved that they stop growing. These severely abused children convert their lack of Love and affection into depleted growth hormone. Chopra states, "In the case of children suffering from psychosocial dwarfism, putting them in a loving environment proves more effective than administering growth hormone (their belief in being unwanted and unworthy can be so strong that their bodies will not grow even when hormones are injected into them). However, if Loving foster parents can transform the children's core belief about being unlovable, they can respond with bursts of naturally produced growth hormone, which sometimes brings them back to normal height, weight and development. When they see themselves differently, their personal reality is altered at a physiological level."[1]

Wow! I read this a few years back and rolled it around in my mind until suddenly, one day, I realized that I'd had a quite similar experience when I was a child. As far as I know my physical growth wasn't stunted and my parents were not knowingly abusive, but I felt severe pain as a result of a deprivation of Love during my childhood.

You see, I was the youngest of four boys in my family and for the first 10 years of my life my parents battled constantly. I don't remember a lot of the specifics because I blocked it out, but I know there was a lot of screaming. The battling officially ended five days before my 10th birthday when my father died of a stroke. His funeral was on my 10th birthday and God only knows how that might have scarred me.

By the time my father died, my two oldest brothers, Mike and John, had moved out of the house. The household now consisted of my mother, my brother Dan and me. Dan's four years older than I am and I found myself spending a lot of time with him while my mother was working. Spending time with him, that is, when he wasn't paying me to get lost. He simply didn't want his little brother around, so he'd throw me a dime or a quarter to make me go away. It also seemed to him that every time that I touched one of his possessions that it got broken. The more he accused me of these things, the more frightened I became. When I was in the presence of any thing that belonged to Dan I became very nervous and quite clumsy. I had become so self conscious that I really couldn't touch his be-longings without breaking them. In psychological terms this represented something referred to as a self-fulfilling prophecy.

This was only the tip of the iceberg in terms of the damage that was being done, however. The real dagger came when my big brother branded me with a nickname that buried itself deep inside of me and affected everything that I did. The nickname was "Worthless." Dan was a teenager at the time and I'm sure that he had no idea how this would impact my life.

So here I was a kid who could add, subtract, multiply and divide, in his

When you give Love away it will not be depleted it comes back ten fold whenever it's needed.

Heart Full of Love

head, faster than anyone I knew at any age. In the 7th grade I weighed 115 pounds and could throw a softball 84 yards. If I could touch a football I could catch it. I had a deadly outside shot on the basketball court, could fake most people out of their jock, and by the time I was 5'7" tall I could jump up and grab a regulation 10-foot basketball rim.

Who would guess that a person with a resume like mine would almost flunk out of school and couldn't make a lay up in front of an audience. I was branded worthless and I lived up to my nickname every time that I performed in front of a crowd. I was so afraid to fail that my fear projected itself into a blueprint for failure. I wanted so badly to succeed because I felt I had to in order to be accepted. I wasn't aware at the time that it was Love that I was seeking. Love was not a frequent topic of discussion in our household. A vicious cycle was occurring. I was screwing everything up because I was unloved and I was unloved because I screwed everything up.

I began to feel like I was dying and I didn't know why. In the search for the answer I started to get clues from TV shows where someone was dying of an obscure disease. That's it, I said, I must have this disease or that disease. I had every new disease that came along and the symptoms to go with it. I was looking for an explanation for why I was dying and I hadn't been taught about Love, so I surely didn't know that you could get sick or die from a lack of it.

This only made matters worse. Now I'd earned a new nickname, "Hypochondriac." It didn't take me long to realize that was not a good thing to be either.

I'm happy to report that I lived through every one of those incurable diseases. I experienced just enough Love along the way to survive. As a kid, I got that Love from my grandmother and my brother Mike, when he would come home from college periodically. They were always glad to see me and made me feel important. In my mid-teens I became pretty popular with the girls and that was my sustenance. In my twenties I realized that my mother was full of Love but didn't know how to show it to those who mattered the most, or perhaps I just hadn't recognized just how Loving she was. In my thirties it was the measure of success, respect and acceptance I had gained in my professional life that filled the void. During my thirties I also began a deep exploration of my spirituality. Now that I'm in my forties I have an extended spiritual family and feel God's Love all around me.

It took me almost 40 years to realize that my symptoms of physical illness were caused by a deficiency of Love, much like psychosocial dwarfism. This awareness has been quite liberating. The label "Worthless" has magically disappeared and I not only forgive my brother, I thank him for this most debilitating blessing. Without it I probably would have never recognized my

The most valuable possession you can own is an open Heart. The most powerful weapon you can be is an instrument of peace.

Carlos Santana

own true worth. Without it I would probably have succeeded only in upholding society's measure of worth, never venturing into the expansive depths of the Heart. I would have never discovered the treasures that lay there. And it is unlikely that I would have developed compassion for others at such great depth. I also probably wouldn't have learned how dangerous it can be to label other human beings.

> *Though what we're seeing*
> *Sometimes hurts us,*
> *All the anger, fear and pain,*
> *They're only rising to the surface*
> *To be replaced with Love again.*[2]

MICHAEL TOMLINSON
"Living Things"

ɣə

VIP Passes

I've mentioned that as a child the thing that got me through was the Love of my grandmother and my oldest brother. I also said that they made me feel important. They were always glad to see me and they were interested in me. They praised the little things I did and they weren't afraid to touch me. Yes, they showed me that I was important and that the things I did were important.

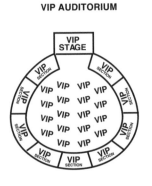

VIP AUDITORIUM

I think that as long as we occupy human bodies that we will have a need for people to listen to us, to pay attention to us and let us know that what we're up to and what we have to say are important to them. If we could see everyone as they truly are, "Very Important Persons," we couldn't help but recognize that we too are VIPs. Once again, if we practice the golden rule, "do unto others as you would have them do unto you," we end up doing unto ourselves as we would have others do unto us.

Almost every social event has a section set aside for VIPs. Usually the section is very small and represents only a minute portion of those in attendance. Does that make everybody else VUPs, Very Unimportant Persons? That's a scary thought, but in our dualistic society that's the underlying implication.

Wouldn't it be great to attend concerts, plays, and ball games where every single person received a ticket that said "VIP Pass" right beside the name of the event? Better still, what if they put up banners in every section that shouted, VIP Section. This would validate the truth, that everyone is a Very Important Person. It would be a great start for something much bigger.

Venture into the depths of the Heart and discover the treasures that lay there.

Narrow The Gap

I recently heard a quote that was attributed to Albert Einstein which seemed to sum up my perception of our progress as a species. Einstein said "our humanity has surpassed our technology." At the time that Dr. Einstein made that statement few households in America had televisions, people performed simple mathematical calculations with a pencil and paper (no calculator) and the only computers were the size of your living room. Those monstrosities could be found only in science labs and were far less efficient than today's average household PC. We've sure come a long way since then, technologically, that is.

I believe that the point that Dr. Einstein was making was that the advancements in science and medicine were out pacing the advancements in matters of the heart. By this I mean such things as peaceful coexistence, compassion and brotherhood (sisterhood too). The golden rule is not practiced any more today than it was in our ancestors' days.

So, as our technology races ahead at breakneck speed, our humanity remains at a standstill, some might even suggest that it's going backwards. I believe we must narrow the gap.

How do we narrow the gap? We can start by changing our priorities. We ought to master the technology we have before we rush ahead to develop new technologies. As we go about that task, we can assess the value of our new gadgets and ask ourselves; does this really improve the quality of my life? Does this help me to strengthen my relationship with my children, my family, my friends? Does it make me a better citizen?

Technology was supposed to be our friend and it can be if we use it properly. Technology used for the sake of profit, at the cost of losing our connection to each other, is too great a price to pay. Our top priority should be to dedicate ourselves to living by the golden rule instead of living under the rule of gold.

Here and Now

The book *Island*,[3] written in 1962 by Aldous Huxley, is a book about a utopian society. This utopia is located on a small island with an independent government, far away from the rest of civilization. On this island everyone is respected for their individual talents. They live simply, efficiently, and Lovingly with reverence to the land, the sea and to each other. They do not lack for education and everyone has a sense of dignity. They have almost no need for prisons or mental institutions. Even their hospitals are small because they practice preventative medicine and a simple lifestyle. One especially unique feature of the island is that everywhere you go there are birds calling to you, "here and now,

We should live by the golden rule instead of living under the rule of gold.

here and now." This is the only language the birds know and a constant reminder to each person to live in the moment and seize the now.

This fictional society provides us with a glimpse of what could be. If we could develop a magic potion that would give everyone an instant sense of dignity, self-Love, and acceptance of all other people, and at the same time take away the ability to live in the past or the future, we would nearly eliminate the need for hospitals, asylums and prisons.

My own personal formula reduces the equation even further, down to these two things:

1. Live entirely in the present moment.

2. Keep Love at the Heart of all action.

Master these things and you will have a Heaven on Earth. Oh, there is one more thing, smile a lot.

If you smile at me I will understand
'Cause a smile is something
Everyone does in the same language.[4]

DAVID CROSBY, STEVEN STILLS
AND PAUL KANTNER
"Wooden Ships"

Heart Full Of Love

Keep a Heart full of Love
And a mind full of joy
Then no other tasks will
You need to employ

Well, smiling's good too
When you do it with Love
It transfers to others
This gift from above

If you give Love away
It will not be depleted
It comes back ten-fold
Whenever it's needed

So your full Heart gets fuller
How can this be?
Love has no limits
So just set it free

And that Love will flourish
Throughout all the land
Your Heart will be full
Your life will be grand

You'll have made a difference
What more could you ask
A Heart full of Love
Our only task

UNITY VILLAGE, MISSOURI, SUMMER 1994

If we dance to the beat
of our heart upon hearts,
we can map our own routes,
we can chart our own charts

The Dance Of Life

"The Dance Of Life" always has been one of my favorite poems, for a lot of reasons, but most of all because it has a celebration theme and is kinda fun. Even the paper that it's on in my poetry book is fun, very colorful with blue and pink hues for a background with waves and clouds and dolphins jumping out of the water. At the bottom of the page where the poem ends with the words, "Dancing together, Dancing as one" there are three dolphins jumping together in a line that looks like what I think dancing dolphins would look like. What I also like about it is that its theme celebrates both our individuality and our oneness at the same time. In general, I think it has excellent balance, one of the most important and effective principles for enjoying a good life.

There's a spark of the
Creator in every living thing
He respects me when I work,
But He so Loves me when I sing.[1]

DAN FOGELBERG
"Magic Every Moment"

He So Loves Me When I Sing

My favorite Bible passage is John Chapter 15, verses 7-17. Here's an excerpt: "These things I have spoken to you, that my joy may be in you, and that your joy may be full." Other places in the New Testament, Jesus said, "I came that they may have life and have it abundantly" and this one "Love your neighbor as yourself." I don't think that Jesus was teaching us these things so that we could score points with God and have a good afterlife. I think He was telling us how to live, right here, right now. I've got news for you (good news at that). If everybody heeded these words and lived according to His teachings, they wouldn't be speculating about what Heaven is like because they'd already be experiencing it right here on Earth.

The picture that most of us have had conveyed to us about Heaven depicts it as a place where there are lots of people hanging out playing harps all the time. Maybe that's why they call it an after-life because nobody sounds like they're really living. In fact, that place sounds very boring and boredom can be Hell.

My perception of Heaven is consistent with the traditional perspective only in that it usually is depicted as a very clean and uncluttered place. Otherwise, the music is a little more lively than harps, there are lots of pretty girls and golf courses everywhere. Your perception of Heaven is probably different than mine. It is available to you right here, right now. You needn't wait to see what is there on the other side. I think these words from Dan Fogelberg's song "Part Of The Plan" sum it all up: "There is no Eden, no Heavenly gates you're gonna make it to one day. All of the answers you seek can be found in dreams that you dream along the way."[2]

One of my favorite albums is Fogelberg's *River of Souls* album. The song "Magic Every Moment" is a very upbeat song from that album that includes these profound lyrics, "You can see forever in a single drop of dew, you can see the same forever if you look down deep inside of you. There's a spark of the creator in every living thing, he respects me when I work but he so Loves me when I sing."[3] Singing, dancing and playing. Isn't it interesting that all these things are normal and natural behaviors for children? Is it any coincidence that Jesus said that you must become as little children to reach the kingdom of Heaven?

Michael, the angel in the movie by the same name, constantly was demonstrating that life was a dance. Once he looked up to the Heavens and thanked God for giving him another chance to come back into a body and have a little fun. Like a child, Michael was fascinated by simple things like the world's largest ball of yarn and the world's largest non-stick frying pan.

If Heaven was actually what we perceived it to be, would there be some

There is no Eden, no Heavenly gates you're gonna make it to one day. All of the answers you seek can be found in dreams that you dream along the way.

Dan Fogelberg

attributes that are common to everyone? The answer is that while we are each beautiful and unique aspects of the creator we also are one in spirit and all yearn for Love, peace and joy.

E Pluribus Unum

The words E Pluribus Unum appear on the face of every U.S. coin. Translated from Latin to English it means "In many, one." The words were written by the framers of the constitution of the United States of America to recognize our strength as a nation of many people, diverse in origin, color and belief, yet "One Nation Under God, indivisible, with liberty and justice for all." The principle and purpose behind the Constitution was to give us all the freedom to think, worship and create our own lives. As long as we abided by the fair laws of the land we were granted complete freedom of expression without need to fear reproach. The principles themselves were a declarations of encouragement to be your wonderful unique self. These guys were really New Age thinkers.

The Constitution of the United States is a marvelous document that seems to have been written by the hand of God. Isn't it amazing that our money has the words "In God we trust," when we live in a misguided nation that has come to worship the paper, instead of the source behind it?

A Great Balancing Act

A successful human being is one who has learned how to live a balanced life. One of the great sages of our time, Dr. Suess, wrote a classic book entitled *Oh, The Places You'll Go* in which he takes you on a journey through life, through tragedy and triumph and in the end he reminds you that "Life's a great balancing act" and if you remember that "You will succeed. (98 and 3/4% guaranteed.)"[4]

Getting out of balance is an easy thing for us humans to do. Sometimes we get too caught up in physical gratification and lose sight of our true nature as spiritual beings. Other times we have our heads so far in the clouds on our spiritual quest that we forget to take care of our body temple. At those times that we have the latter challenge it would serve us to remember that our body is a temple of God and in taking care of the body we are taking care of the temple that houses our spirit.

I do believe that we are spiritual beings having a physical experience but this physical experience is an important one and we need our bodies to carry out our mission. Alan Cohen talks about how we sometimes go to extremes in our curiosity with non-physical reality in his book *A Deep Breath Of Life*. Someone asked him what percentage of his friends have had out-of-body experiences and he answered, "I know quite a few people who have yet to have an in-body experience."[5]

Life is a great balancing act.
You will succeed.
(98 and 3/4% guaranteed.)

Dr. Suess

Another aspect of balance is the balance between tapping into our inherent childlike innocence and the healthy adult attributes of wisdom and discipline. We need to blend and balance the child and the adult to become whole beings.

Deepak Chopra emphasizes the balance between stillness and movement in his book *The Seven Spiritual Laws Of Success.* Chopra states, "When you quietly acknowledge this exquisite coexistence of opposites, you align yourself with the world of energy...the combination of movement and stillness enables you to unleash your creativity in all directions–wherever the power of your attention takes you."[6]

Finally, there is the balance between the Heart and the mind. It has been said that the longest 18 inches in the world is the expanse between the Heart and the mind. While I associate the Heart with Love and believe that Love is the most important thing in the world, the Heart must be in partnership with the mind for discernment to make the best choices for the whole of our being.

Classroom of Life

One of the most commonly asked philosophical questions of life is, "Is the course of my life predetermined or do I have the free will to make my own choices?" The answer is yes, to both. I have come to believe that there are beautiful parallels between the classroom of life and the classrooms that we sit in to receive our formal education, most especially the college setting.

In college, no matter what your major is, there are many qualifications you must meet before you can graduate. The course of study is broken into two parts, courses you are required to take and courses you can take just because you want to. The latter group of courses are called electives. In life, we also have a certain number of required courses and a certain number of electives.

Some of the obvious required courses include eating and sleeping. These things are required of everyone. The other requirements are likely to be related to the type of body you have inherited (male or female, big or small) and the type of culture you are born into. The requirements to adapt to the culture in the Amazon jungles are quite different than those required to adapt to the jungles of New York City. Some of the obvious electives are whether you're going to have a burger and fries or whether you're going to go for the veggie delight. Once again your body type and culture often determine the electives that are available to you, but you will always have many. Sometimes those choices (electives) have painful consequences but often they prove to be the most rewarding.

Spiritual growth often comes when we make decisions not to conform to

Add another partner, God, and we can create an infinite number of beautiful things.

the wishes of the tribe (our culture). That generally means that you will end up having to deal with the nonacceptance issue, an issue that can leave you feeling very alone. If you stay committed to spirit, sooner or later you'll notice that God is right there beside you, applauding your decision and you will feel alone no more.

The classroom of life presents a medley of many different human experiences. Human beings are a medley of chemical reactions, electrical impulses and independent will, all acting in an interactive partnership that influences each one's individual makeup. If we take this medley and add another partner, God, we can use our classroom experiences to create an infinite number of beautiful things.

Co-Co-Creation

A well-known and popular term these days is *co-creation*. Co-creation refers to forming a partnership with God to create the best life we can. Jesus actually taught us that the easiest way to bring God into the equation was to join together with other people in His name. When we join our intentions it strengthens our creative connection to God. So it's not just me and God, it's me and you and God. This new combination in which we are most mightily empowered has a new coefficient making it Co-Co-Creation. If we gather together in Jesus' name we'll be practicing the art of Love. Loving God. Loving your neighbor. Loving yourself.

You Again?

I've only recently come to believe in reincarnation in the traditional sense, that is, that we reincarnate right here on Earth with a different human body for each lifetime. For most of my life I have believed that the traditional perception of reincarnation was possible but that there were an infinite number of alternate possibilities, other planets, other dimensions, the traditional view of Heaven, etc. I still believe that there are an infinite number of possibilities. However, I have come to believe that the popular theory actually makes the most sense.

If you accept and understand the classroom concept it's easy to see how it would fit the traditional reincarnation theory. For instance, if we were not taught to develop language skills, then learn to read and write, we would not be able to advance from grade to grade. More specifically, if we had not studied our chemistry and obtained the proper undergraduate training we would be clueless as to what to do if we suddenly showed up in a graduate level chemistry course. The same would apply to our consecutive incarnations. The reason that we come back to this place is to master the challenges that we didn't master the last time. There are far too many to handle

We are most mightily empowered when we add a new coefficient making it Co-Co-Creation.

in one lifetime, so when we come into each incarnation there are many life situations that we have mastered on this familiar turf (key term, familiar turf) already. This time we can focus our time, energy and intentions on the things we didn't master before. What happens when we've mastered them all? Haven't got that far yet.

In the movie *Defending Your Life,* the characters get to go hang out with a bunch of counselors who evaluate their lives and determine whether they will be sent back to Earth or not. The counselors were Beings with increased brain capacity (some used more than 50% of their brains) to present the case in a life review for recently deceased "little brains," Earthlings with a 3-5% brain capacity. The stars, Meryl Streep (Julia) and Albert Brooks (Daniel), only had to demonstrate that they had conquered fear and they wouldn't have to go back to Earth.

Julia passed with flying colors as she was shown in one heroic life-review scene after another. The highlight was when she ran into a raging fire to save the family dog. Daniel, on the other hand, was shown in numerous acts of cowardice. Between "trials" Daniel and Julia began to fall in Love, but it looked like they were going to receive two different verdicts and hence would be going in different directions. After it had appeared that the final verdicts had been reached, Julia boarded her vehicle to the next level while Daniel boarded the bus back to Earth, shackled like a prisoner. Somehow Daniel summoned superhuman courage and strength to break free and endured great pain as he would let nothing stop him from reaching his Julia. This incident was being reviewed by his "jury" and they reversed their decision. Daniel was allowed to join Julia on the journey to the next level.

The movie did not reveal their destination but it is an interesting and fun portrayal of what might be. Almost all truth seekers will relate to the need to overcome fear to advance spiritually. In this movie that was the single thing that the characters had to master. Perhaps if we could truly master the art of Love, we would inherently master fear and transcend all other limitations simultaneously.

Envy Of the Galaxy

America is the perfect model for freedom, according to the definition ascribed to by many in today's spiritual movement. What makes it so ideal is because many of the things we must do to maintain our constitutional freedoms very closely parallel the requirements to maintain our spiritual freedom.

Failure to obtain certain licenses, obey speed limits, pay taxes, etc. will ultimately result in meeting resistance from a regulatory authority. That resistance will inhibit our flow and hence our freedom. In the most profound sense we could even be physically imprisoned.

The spiritual mantra is "the truth will set you free" and that's reality, that's the law.

The same laws apply to our relationship with Spirit. If we fail to obtain certain licenses (according to our agreement with God), obey speed limits (our pace of life is at the core of stress and hence most disease) or pay our taxes (karmic debt), we will create limiting factors in our physical, mental, emotional and spiritual lives.

Even our concept of the ultimate enforcing power is similar. In America many people fear an invisible entity called "Big Brother." Big Brother represents the U.S. Government. In our spiritual lives many people live according to a fear of God. If you were to ask people to close their eyes and imagine the two figures, Big Brother and God, they would often draw the same image in their mind.

Both the fear of God and the fear of Big Brother are irrational fears. I know people who are terrorized by the thought that Big Brother is watching over them, and knows what they're up to. So what if he is watching you? If you are playing by the rules, Big Brother won't hurt you. The same applies to God. As long as you're living according to spiritual laws and doing your best, he'll be in your corner.

We just can't get away with breaking the law, so why do people try? It must go back to conditioning. The American mantra is "nice guys finish last." The spiritual mantra is "the truth will set you free" and that's reality, that's the law.

So there you have it. America is the perfect model for the thing that we all seek, freedom. It's the perfect system. It must be the ultimate training school in the whole universe. The envy of a million galaxies and I get to attend here on a full scholarship. Thank you God!

Know Your Vehicle

In a period of about two weeks, I met with two people, of opposite view points, who both listened intently as I shared with them the things that were going on in my life. Both freely offered their perception of my values and advised me as to the course of action I should take to improve my life. One, an old friend who was a newly made millionaire, was adamant that I should take a more proactive approach to making money. The other, a new friend who was nearly penniless, but content, thought that I was too concerned with the comforts of life. My financial status falls between the two, leaning heavily toward the latter individual. They both seem to be content with their situation and I honor where they stand, but neither of their formulas felt right to me. The following journal notes are dedicated to Vernon and Raul.

If you try to force yourself to be someone you're not, the road may be needlessly long and difficult.

> *Many roads often lead to the same place. Pick the one that most suits your vehicle. If your makeup is like a Ferrari, rev your engine and take the Autobahn to your destination. For the rugged sort, grind it out over that rough terrain in your all terrain vehicle. This may allow you to take the most direct route. For the more delicate soul, the smooth route may be best and your choice may be*

to go by the river and allow the current to carry you along. Perhaps the wind is your best choice as you glide on your aerolight, taking in the sights below. On the ground find a smooth road and drive at the pace that suits your vehicle comfortably.

One of the most important lessons you can learn is to know yourself and be yourself. If you try to force yourself to be someone you're not, the road may be needlessly long and difficult.

Don't Be Afraid To Doodle

Everyone has a unique creative side to them. It just shows up differently for different people. Don't be afraid to experiment with things that suit your creative fancy. You never know what beautiful creation may appear. I'm lousy at drawing but I know that I can doodle. Sometimes, with a little help, that doodling turns into something really good. Here's a before and after on one that I'm pretty proud of. (For the "after" doodle see page 168).

My journal is usually the canvas for the beginning of my masterpiece. Before I make my first brush strokes (since I'm using a pen I might be stretching it a little) I carefully contemplate the image that I want to create. Then I put my thoughts into words and my words onto the paper. Finally, I'm ready to put on my artist (doodler) hat. I set my brush (pen) to the canvas (journal) and commence to doodle.

Here's an unedited, real life example from my journal on July 13, 1997:

> *"I walked the rails to Lake Lily. There I found a forked stick that looked like a wishbone. I thought I'd keep it at home and make wishes for good things, like more Love, less fear. I sat down by the lake and looked at a tree that looked like a fork until I put the wish stick up in its visual field and noticed that the branches plumped out and curled like a Heart."*

To thine own self be true. William Shakespeare

Then I imagined the illustration that appears on the next page.

This way to the illustration...

Another doodle waiting for an artist.

Heart   Wishbone

I wish peoples Hearts would fill with Love to replace the fear.

I broke the wishbone.

It's a good start.

The wishbone actually did break just before I got home

Don't Be Afraid To Doodle

Have no fear doodle here!

Havin' Fun Yet?

Singer Jimmy Buffet generally is recognized as a fun guy. One of the most memorable quotes comes from his song "Changes In Latitudes, Changes In Attitudes" in which he cautions us not to take life too seriously, with the following, "With all of the islands and all of the highlands, if we couldn't laugh we would all go insane."[7]

With this idea in mind, I'm going to share with you some of the things that I have done to break the tension. The key here is to apply the same spiritual laws to tension busters as anything else. If it feels like a good idea and you're not going to hurt anyone's feelings, shake off the fear that the tribe won't approve, and just do it. Here are a few simple examples of some of the things that I have done to open up the silly side of me and open "a new dimension, free from tension."

Cocka Doodle Doo

Once my friend Cat was lying on the couch and told me that her foot was asleep. Being the helpful kind of a guy that I am, I went and got my battery powered alarm clock, turned on the ringer and set it down right in front of her foot. She laughed so hard that I couldn't figure out if it woke her foot up or if she had just forgotten about it.

Chinese Zodiac

I've found that the answering machine is an excellent place to share inspiring thoughts. At the first of the year I put a message on the answering machine related to the Chinese Zodiac. I got the information from a placemat that I picked up at a Chinese restaurant. The year (1997) was the year of the Ox and I shared some of this ancient Oriental Wisdom via the answering machine.

It was incredible the number of comments that people made about the warning to all Ox that Sheep were trouble and that they should marry a Snake. Numerous women disputed the advice about marrying a Snake, saying that they had tried that in a previous marriage and it hadn't worked out.

Totally Serious Golf

I saw a bumper sticker a while back that said "Life's a game, golf is serious." Being a golfer at Heart (I don't play much), I certainly know the game and know just how many people take it very seriously. Golf is a game of etiquette. You dress nattily and remain totally still and quiet when a golfer is preparing to hit his or her shot.

One fine day, a few years back, my three playing partners and I spontaneously decided to change the rules completely and turned a round of golf into a silly experience of almost uninterrupted laughter that lasted for 18 holes (about 4 hours).

A new dimension, free from tension.

One of the great pranksters and most fun loving persons I know, Robbie Stewart, had set our tee time and we met his brother Scott, also a character, at the golf course.

Even though we didn't plan it this way, we knew it was going to be different when a stranger joined our group to round out the foursome and proceeded to lose all four of his golf balls on the first hole. That's not normally funny, but Ken, our new playing partner, had set himself up prior to teeing off, when he asked us if we thought he had enough balls to play (he meant the whole round).

At some point early on in the round, one of my partners intentionally made noise in the middle of my back swing and I dubbed the shot. He apologized and allowed me to hit over, only to do it again, causing me to mess up again. This time it drew a few chuckles and the games had begun. We left our new playing partner out of it but every time that Robbie, Scott or I were hitting a shot, throats were being cleared or clubs were being clanged. Then there was the ever favorite putting the cart in reverse thus causing a loud buzzer to go off. I would whiff the ball I was laughing so hard and everyone else was roaring. Once in a while it was quiet. That would throw us off as we waited for the noise that never came.

Toward the end of the round, I began to plan a surprise, a touch of the bizarre. I was going to throw my rusty golf clubs, that I was planning on replacing right away, in the lake. It was designed to portray a fit of disgust as no one knew about the condition of my clubs or my true motive.

On the signature hole, the par three 17th hole–

which features an island green–I hit my ball in the lake, took my bag off the cart and yelled "I can't take this game anymore!" I proceeded to throw my inexpensive, rusty clubs in the lake (I kept my golf bag and my woods which I had sneaked into Robbie's golf bag). My normally zany friends actually thought that I had gone a little too far until I explained that I had been scheming it for a while. It brought more laughter as we went out with a bang.

Many golfers may be cringing as they read this, but I highly recommend that you try "totally serious golf" sometime. It will help you to remember that golf is just a game after all.

Magic Carpet Ride

In another spur of the moment, "Carpe Diem" move, we decided that we'd go to the airport and greet the home team as they returned home from their final game of the 1996-97 season.

The home team, the Orlando Magic, had a controversial, roller coaster ride for a season and entered the playoffs as a mystery team. After losing the first two games of their best-of-five playoff series, they had drawn massive criticism from everyone, sportswriters and fans alike, mostly because they seemed not to care or have any Heart. They

Hope exists when you put your Heart before your reason.

surprised everyone by winning games three and four which forced a series–deciding fifth game, to be played in the lair of the Miami Heat's home arena. Overmatched and playing against great odds, the Magic fell behind but never gave up. They gave their fans hope, time after time, when their Hearts pushed them past reason. Each time that they looked like they were beaten they would pull close due to incredible plays and hustle from even the most unlikely players.

In the end, the Heat had won the game and advanced in the playoffs, but the Magic had won our Hearts, most of them, anyway.

As soon as the game was over, I announced that I wanted to go to the airport and show my appreciation to the team for reclaiming their Hearts and opening ours. To welcome the home team we made a large poster/ sign that said:

"THE HEARTS OF CHAMPIONS–
WE LOVE YOU!!!"

Right in the middle we drew a big red Heart and pasted the Magic logo inside it.

At the airport, as we were celebrating this magical spontaneous experience of life, to our delight a man came out to the fenced security area and gave us flight arrival updates and handed us pins in the shape of wings with the company's logo "Magic Carpet Aviation."

In the end, we did this to celebrate the team for what they were, the champions of our Hearts. On this day the rest of the season wasn't important, all that mattered was the way the team ended it.

Little experiences like this can whisk us away on a Magic Carpet Ride to a Heavenly place in our Hearts.

Life is what happens
When we are
Busy making other plans.

JOHN LENNON

❧

Pollinating

In a way, this is an aspect of my new approach to living my life, new in 1997, by pollinating the world with Love as often as I can. Beginning in January of 1997, every time I would leave the house I would leave armed with my latest poem or other inspirational words, a spirit of adventure, curiosity and an open Heart. My morning walks, my stops for coffee and a bagel, and all my shopping experiences were the perfect opportunities to pollinate the world with Love. Sometimes, I'd give away poetry, sometimes it was Mardi Gras beads, other times just a smile and a blessing. I almost always made new friends, giving and receiving blessings all along the way.

Follow the voice of your own Heart.

BELIEVE IN HOPE
LIVE YOUR
DREAM

You could say that 1997 was a defining year for me, one where my spirit came to know its own flight pattern. Many of my demons of fear were slain and I was blessed with God's abundant Grace. By Grace I have continued to journey the length of the light. Along the way, my pathway has been illumined by this brilliant light. I am becoming adept at hearing and following the voice of my own Heart. The voice of my Heart delivers a clear message consistent with my favorite button that says "Believe in hope, live your dream." I have deepened my faith and as I act upon it I have been shown the Grace of God.

I've entered a new era, one in which I hope to continue pollinating the planet with Love and teaching others to do the same. From now on I intend to celebrate the dance of life in every situation. I will celebrate my own unique gifts and I'll be celebrating yours. And I will celebrate our oneness. Dance with me, won't you?

Wealthy the Spirit that
Knows its own flight,
Stealthy the hunter
Who slays his own fright,
Blessed the traveler
Who journeys the length of the light.[8]

DAN FOGELBERG
"Nexus"

••• Ⓢ •••

The Dance Of Life

To the Dance of Life we've all come to engage
We all have our own rhythms
We all have our own stage

We can dance with joy
Or we can dance with sorrow
Or we can choose a new dance
With each new tomorrow

If we dance to the beat of
Our Heart upon Hearts
We can map our own routes
We can chart our own charts

We can soar in the Heavens
While angels draw near
With God as our co-pilot and nothing to fear

When we come back to Earth
We can share what we know
And with this new knowledge
Help others to grow
And spread their own wings
And join us in flight
Enriched with new wisdom
Blessed with clear sight

Dancing together, dancing as one
In celebration of life
Thy will be done

LAKE IVANHOE, ORLANDO, FLORIDA, WINTER 1994

*When one chooses as their occupation,
Professional Human Being,
they use the tools that they are equipped with
to become happy while being committed to
doing good and not doing harm.*

Occupation: Professional Human Being

I had the good fortune to meet Peter Carlson during one of my life assignments in which I wore a label called "Executive Director of The Loren Quinn Institute, A Center For Attitudinal Healing." Peter was the person who came up with the concept of the Professional Human Being (PHB). I decided to write about the concept and put a definition with it that would express my personal intentions as well as honor the teachings of Peter Carlson.

Peter's main side job is in the Mental Health profession as a counselor. He also taught a series of ongoing meditation classes at Loren Quinn, which quite frankly, were what allowed the center to keep on going. You see, Peter did the classes as a benefit and each 4-6 week class generated about $500 for the center.

Peter used a grease board and drew some great illustrations on the subject of brain function and how different states of mind produced different chemical reactions in the brain and other really cool stuff. But most of all Peter taught us how to breathe, how to sit, and how to be mindful. In fact, Peter rarely used the term meditation. He simply referred to the practice of sitting.

To be mindful is to pay attention, to be awake and aware of life and all of the magical things that are going on around you and inside of you. Peter has been dedicated to the practice of meditation for more than 20 years now and is so mindful and interested in life that he claims that he never gets bored. And the real good news is that he always has a very peaceful countenance. I think he wears it well, inside and out.

The Costumes We Wear

To say that I am a professional human being is certainly a testimony to the only title that I am striving to maintain. Not that this title, as I have defined it, is an easy one to live up to. However, it's the only title/costume that I feel comfortable wearing.

I learned a long time ago that every title or designation is just another label that we use to identify ourselves with and carries an expectation of behavior associated with it. When I graduated from college with a degree in Psychology, I discovered that there were people who were afraid that I was going to psychoanalyze them. In truth, I only had a bachelor's degree. At the time, in 1980, there was little room in the psychological community for someone with the philosophical whimsy and spiritual curiosity that I had. In short, nothing that I had learned in the classroom made me any more dangerous in the sense that I might recognize and reveal someone's pathological condition that they would just as soon keep a secret.

Labels are not a bad thing as long as we don't generalize behaviors. Labels are a fine thing so long as we can differentiate and realize that underneath that label or title lies a Divine combination of body, mind and spirit, packaged in its own unique form.

Professional Human Being

The flip side of one of my business cards has this condensed description of a "Professional Human Being," as a quick and easy way to identify myself when someone asks, "What do you do for a living?"

Be awake to all of the magical things that are going on around you and inside of you.

A Professional Human Being
(PHB)
uses the marvelous instrumentation
of the brain combined with the
Divine aspect of the Heart
to make choices that best suit the
objective of bringing happiness
while doing good and not doing harm.

What Do You Do For A Living?

I've always hated the question and right now it's harder than ever to answer. So, to make things easy for me and give folks a satisfactory explanation of what I "do for a living," I made up one of these:

What Do You Do For A Living?

Current Update for Jeff Tressler
March 9, 1997

1. Professional Human Being

(There are two sides to this card, check it out) This is what I consider to be my true occupation, it's the real me. It's a tough reputation to live up to, but I cherish the assignment. All of the other cards simply represent a costume that I wear.

Jeff Tressler, P.H.B.
PROFESSIONAL HUMAN BEING

1-800 CARPE DIEM

2. Krewe of Paradians

Speaking of costumes, I dress up in a jester outfit, with a hat like the one on the card for this job. I'm using my skills mentioned in card #4 to help bring the Mardi Gras to Orlando. Right now the boss pays me with massages.

Krewe of Paradians

Jeff Tressler
events coordinator

P.O. Box 3
Orlando, FL 32802

3. Mears Transportation Group

This is the one that is currently paying the bills. I dress in a coat and tie and chauffeur people from luxury hotels to restaurants, attractions and the airport. The car I drive is not quite a limo, it's a white Lincoln towncar.

M MEARS TRANSPORTATION GROUP
Group Transportation Professionals Since 1939
324 W. Gore Street, Orlando, FL 32806, Reservations (407) 423-5566

Jeffrey Tressler
DRIVER # 81436

4. Communication Consultant

This one is still on the drawing board but is developing into a way for me to use my real talents to bring me real dollars. This job lines up with the PHB because the skills come naturally. I don't have to pretend, my costume is me.

• Proposals
• Newsletters & Brochures
• Dispute Resolution
• Copywriting

Jeff Tressler
Communication Consultant
Language Artistry

GET TO THE HEART OF THE MATTER
FROM BUSINESS LETTERS TO SONNETS

The EEK-omomy

Naturally the reason that everyone is so concerned with what everybody else does for a living is because most of us aren't creative enough to ask a more interesting question. When people ask you, "what do you do for a living?", they are usually trying to get a handle on how much money you make. Money, how much of it you have and how much everyone else has, is a very important thing in America. Because people are concerned about money they're usually very concerned about something called "the state of our economy."

The dictionary is a beautiful thing. If you go to the dictionary and look up economy you realize that it has nothing to do with what we think it does. More accurately, it has nothing to do with what we are conditioned to believe it does. The word economy is not about big bucks and big spending. Quite the contrary. Economy actually is much like efficiency – the ratio of energy expended to energy gained.

The thing that we think of as our economy is entirely misnamed. We consider our economy to be this huge, complex machine that makes no sense whatsoever. That which is supposed to be the gauge by which our economic

I'm a Professional Human Being, I just take side jobs to pay the bills.

Peter Carlson

health, as a nation, is measured, is something called the stock market. Here's an example of how confusing this animal is: *NEWS BULLETIN: The stock market dropped today on news that new home sales are at an all time high, raising fears that the Feds will boost interest rates.* What? Owning your own home is the American dream, how can that be bad news?

The economy and the stock market are things that most Americans are very concerned about. They were so concerned back in 1929 when the stock market crashed that scores of people were testing the law of gravity by jumping off very tall buildings. This kind of concern is not healthy.

If people were concerned about real economy and lived their lives according to its true principle, then they would find that it fits in very well with natural and spiritual laws.

By the way, Funk and Wagonall's defines economy thusly, "disposition to save or spare; carefulness in outlay, freedom from extravagance and waste, frugality." You won't find any "Wall Street Journal" reports celebrating frugality and carefulness. Spending makes the market twist and shout, not saving and sparing.

As I contemplated the idea of sparing, not wasting, I realized that we are beginning to do this because our "economy" blew so many resources on extravagances (see definition for contradiction). We now are blessed to learn what economy really is. We get to learn that one loaf can feed the masses. We get to learn about simplicity and we get to learn how to share.

Heaven and Hell

There is a well known story that uses a metaphor to help distinguish between Heaven and Hell. Alan Cohen tells it like this: "A man was being given a tour of the kingdoms beyond this world. His guide opened a door where he saw a group of unhappy people standing around a sumptuous banquet. Although the tables were spread with inviting, delicious food, the people were starving. When the man looked closer, he saw that the spoons that the people were holding were longer than their arms, and they could not get food into their mouths. 'This,' the guide explained, 'is Hell.'

"Then show me Heaven," the man requested.

"The guide opened another door where another group of people were standing before a similar banquet with spoons longer than their arms. In this room, however, the people were happy and their tummies were full. The people in Heaven had learned to feed one another."[1]

It is my theory that we'll learn to feed each other, one way or another, as it will be necessary for survival of the species. Instead of survival of the fittest, we are living in an era of survival of the kindest. Ross Perot has

We are living in an era of survival of the kindest.

made the point and backed it up statistically that American wages are worth far less than they were a generation ago. That's not necessarily good news but it's not necessarily bad news either. People in America are learning new values and are having to turn to each other to meet their needs.

Eventually, I think that this will lead us forward to live in interdependent communities where the sharing of our time, talents and treasures will unite us and cooperation will be the pillar on which our society stands.

Native American traditions have become very popular lately. These are traditions in which the people honored the land, its creatures and each other. Children were celebrated as the light of the world and were nurtured through all the stages of their lives. The elderly were just that, the elders, and were looked upon with reverence and respect as they were turned to to guide the tribe by the compass of their wisdom. Unlike contemporary America, where the young are taught to be seen but not heard and old people are put out to pasture, these people all knew how to feed each other. No one was left out because of their age.

Occupational Hazard

Now that I've gotten real heavy, I would like to return to a subject more related to the economy, especially the aspect of our occupations.

The opening inspiration for this segment comes from my fellow Floridian, Jimmy Buffet. In his classic song "A Pirate Looks At Forty" he says, "Mother, Mother Ocean after all the years I've found my occupational hazard is, my occupation's just not around."[2] I've struggled with finding an occupation that suits me all my life. To correct that matter, I just went ahead and made up an "Occupational License." I had it nicely framed for my wall, so that I could "legally" practice being a Professional Human Being.

You see, when it came to finding a job, most of my life I've fallen into one of two categories, I was either under-qualified or overqualified. In the jobs where I was over qualified I offered to tie one hand behind my back, but that never got me hired. I just never could fit into these cookie cutter positions that our mechanized world demands.

Actually, I did do quite nicely as building manager/leasing agent/marketing director. It was a position that allowed me to use my communication skills in a wide variety of ways to engineer "win-win outcomes in the business world" (snippet from my resume). However, I felt too confined, and eventually burned out on corporate politics.

The perfect job for me, and one for which I am totally qualified, is connoisseur of fine beaches. I have sampled many, most of them right here in my home state. I offer you these journal notes from May 13, 1994, to demonstrate to you my qualifications.

Children were celebrated as the light of the world and were nurtured through all the stages of their lives.

I am going to become a connoisseur of fine beaches. After I have surveyed beaches all around the planet and evaluated their peculiarities, of course, staying as a dignitary at each location, I will write a best selling book on the subject.

Destin (Florida) does indeed have a world class beach. Too many high rises, but a world class beach. The sand is a sparkling white powder. The waves are quite noisy for a Gulf side beach. The reason for this is that they are rushing in so rapidly, small waves, one right after the other. As you look out into the water for the first 50 yards, you see the gorgeous emerald green water that these beaches are indeed famous for. The water is very clear as you'll notice when you get right down on top of it. Very clear, staying very shallow for a long way out.

If you're out there reading this and you've been looking for someone to fill this position, I'm your man.

Professionally Speaking

We are not the costumes that we wear and often not the behaviors that we engage in. To spend our lives trying to uphold an image that society deems as worthy is a sad way to spend this brief spin around the block. We should be fully alive during every moment of the ride. If we could recapture the curiosity of the child that still resides within us we would discover that there is magic and wonder all around us and realize that we have been unwittingly duped by our tribe. We have been duped into believing that the title we wear is who we are and that is what is important.

Be willing to change costumes. Realize that they are all costumes and that even the most beautiful one is not as beautiful as the real you. If you can remember that about yourself and apply this understanding when you look at another human being, you will be taking a very important step in reclaiming spirit and opening a door to rejoin the human race.

Claim your degree as a Professional Human Being and ultimately you will discover a much bigger and more beautiful world.

· · · ⊛ · · ·

Even the most beautiful costume is not as beautiful as the real you.

Occupational License

This certificate,
acknowledged by God
as the witness and under His authority,
hereby appoints:

Professional Human Being

Sworn to be mindful and
dedicated to the following oath:

*To the best of my God given ability,
I will combine and balance the marvelous
instrumentation of the brain
with the Divine aspect of the Heart to
make choices that best suit the objective
of bringing happiness
while doing good and not doing harm.*

Effective from this date until the end of time.

_____
Date

_____
Angelic Representative

Occupation:
Professional Human Being

When one chooses as their occupation,
"Professional Human Being" (PHB),
they choose to use the tools that they are equipped
with to become happy while being committed to
doing good and not doing harm.

The PHB must just BE quite often. They observe the
wonder all around them with all of their senses.
They are curious but not nosey.

They are curious about such things as their emotions
but do not judge them. If the emotion feels painful,
they observe the emotion and let it go.

The Professional Human Being will encounter fear
like any other human being but will observe it
and remember that almost all fears are
based upon something that does not exist.
Most fears are based on fantasy and illusion.
A PHB knows that.

Professional Human Beings know that they will be
confronted with choices almost continuously.
A PHB will use the marvelous instrumentation of the
brain combined with the Divine aspect of the Heart to
make choices that best suit the objective of bringing
happiness while doing good and not doing harm.

In the world of spirit
only love abides,
it has no conditions,
it never derides

World Of Spirit

In Stevie Wonder's classic song, "Ebony and Ivory," he uses the following metaphor: "Ebony and Ivory, live together in perfect harmony, side by side on my piano, oh Lord why don't we?"[1]

These lyrics pose one of the great questions of our time, why is there still so much racial strife in America, and the world for that matter? Of course, there are many reasons for this, historical reasons, cultural reasons and most of all, lack of reason. That is, lack of a proper reasoning faculty.

Just a few minutes before sitting down to type this, I was standing on a dock over looking a lake. I was looking out over the water and watching the birds who were particularly active. Many different types of birds were all doing some sort of dance together. Then I glanced back at the shore and was taken by the diversity of plant life – reeds, lily pads and cattails. Standing side by side were a maple tree and a pine tree. Their leaves couldn't be any more different. The pine tree doesn't have leaves at all. It has long, fine green needles, and the maple tree has big broad leaves. A little further down the shoreline stands a banana tree with the biggest leaves of all, standing next to a weeping willow that has drooping branches and green tinsel-like stuff instead of leaves. It all sounds pretty great doesn't it? One of the main reasons that it sounds so good is because it's describing something called variety. People spend a year's savings to travel to someplace where the scenery and the culture are different but go to great lengths to avoid the different subcultures that exist within their own culture. "Variety is the spice of life" is a saying with which we are all familiar and most folks would agree with. As a society, it appears that this principle applies to everything but the people in our own neighborhood.

> *Talk about your country,*
> *There's really no such thing for me.*
> *The whole world is one big family.*[2]

CARLOS SANTANA
"Give and Take"

ℰ๑

Colored Entrance In Rear

Having grown up, for the most part, in the South, I have been exposed to a great deal of overt racial prejudice. While I have witnessed the energy going in both directions, I've only been privy to the overt displays and statements as they apply to the white bigotry toward blacks.

We moved to Florida from Ohio just before my 11th birthday. My mother had strongly instilled in us that the color of a person's skin was no indicator of the "content of their character." When I made my first visit to the doctor's office shortly after we moved here, there was a baffling sign on the front door which read "Colored entrance in rear." Translation, blacks had to go around to the back and go into their own private waiting room so that they wouldn't offend the white folks in the front.

Those kinds of signs are long gone, at least in my neighborhood. However, while race relations are nowhere near where they should be by now, I personally think that we are stalling the process of improving them by continuing to focus on what's wrong. The leaders of the oppressed and the formerly oppressed should stand up and say hallelujah for the progress that we've made and proclaim "we've still got a long way to go, but we've also come a long way, so let's get together and plant some more good seeds and till this fertile soil together." Focusing on the bad stuff just fuels the fire, keeping us stuck and at odds with each other.

The white man always has made the rules in this country, up to now, and they have been stinky rules, but that is changing. In making these observations I'm going out on a limb a little bit but I am sticking to my spiritual

Let's get together and plant some more good seeds and till this fertile soil together.

principles. Whatever we focus our attention on is what we attract. If we keep focusing on what is wrong we will stay mired in separation. If we focus on what is right we can build bridges instead of burning them. For those who don't buy the spiritual perspective, we can turn to good old behavioral science. You'd be hard pressed to find a social scientist today who would dispute the notion that the best way to promote creativity, self esteem and productivity is through positive reinforcement and encouragement. Encouragement makes us shine; discouragement makes us dull.

I consider Martin Luther King the greatest role model of my lifetime. He rallied thousands of people to march in peaceful demonstration against the atrocities of racism. Everywhere they marched they encountered resistance, but they did not resist.

It was through the spiritual law of non-resistance that Martin Luther King paved the way for blacks to not only sit in the waiting rooms with whites, but for scores of them to get the education and acceptance that would not have otherwise been available. Now, many black doctors have waiting rooms of their own to treat whites and blacks alike. On August 28, 1963, Dr. King delivered his famous "I Have a Dream" address, saying, "I have a dream that one day on the red hills of Georgia the sons of former slaves and the sons of former slaveowners will be able to sit together at the table of brotherhood."[3]

Do we dare say that Dr. King's dream was just an illusion? If he were here today, do you think that he would feel encouraged by the progress that has been made toward making his dreams come true? I think he would. Would he be satisfied? I doubt that he would be happy about the inhumanity that is still prevalent between the races. Should we be satisfied? No way.

So what do we do? Well, spiritual law is God's law and we are all God's children regardless of race, creed or color. Spiritual law and Jesus' commandment is to *Love one another.* There is your answer. You need look no further than this.

Blessing in a Major Disguise

By my 39th birthday in October of 1993, I was ready for a radical change in my life that would require that I make a few leaps of faith. I was eager to leave the so called security of my $50,000 a year position to pursue a vocation that, in my words, "would allow me to serve God full time, not just after hours." I wanted to have my own ministry, a ministry based upon the premise that we could allow Love, joy and peace to guide our lives. I wasn't sure what that ministry would look like or where my pulpit would be, but I was pretty confident that God would show me the way.

By the spring of 1994, after having made my second trip to the world headquarters for Unity Churches in

If we focus on what is right we can build bridges instead of burning them.

Unity Village, Missouri, it looked like a most Divine plan had unfolded for me. I had met someone there that I was convinced was my soulmate who had professed the same feelings for me. We had decided that I would move there, live with her and work in the prayer room at Silent Unity.

By July 2nd, I had packed my car and gone to the airport to pick up the girl of my dreams and have a little honeymoon trip back to Missouri. We'd take our time, hang out at the beach, make Love and be blissful.

Within 48 hours, my brain was flashing a neon sign that said YOU FOOL. Cathy was challenging me and finding fault with everything that I did. She wasn't ready for me and I certainly wasn't ready for this kind of reception.

I did, however, move to Unity Village and Cathy and I lived together for almost eight months. We grew together and often it seemed like we were really in Love. There were also too many times that we needed a referee.

I came home to Florida for Christmas of '94. During that time I applied for the job of my dreams, running a center for Attitudinal Healing, a place that was founded on the 12 most beautiful guiding principles I had ever heard.

In January, I was offered the job and an opportunity to return home to the warmth and sunshine of my beloved Florida.

I was back home now, 1400 miles away from Cathy. However, just like the girl of my dreams, the job of my dreams was not what it appeared to be. It was consumed by politics and egos. I remained baffled as to what had happened to those wonderful principles. I couldn't get off the roller coaster ride. I was longing to have my old life back, the life that I had taken years to build and thrown away in a second. By the spring of 1996, the job of my dreams had turned into the job of my nightmares.

On July 1st, my car was packed and I was off, alone this time, to visit the "Village of Harmony," my friend Mike's self-sufficient community in the desert, 50 miles south of Albuquerque, New Mexico. It was here that I realized once and for all that I had fallen into the pit of Hell. While the community was an impressive monument to simplicity and innovation, the New Mexican desert in the middle of July was no place for a Florida boy who would rather be at the ocean than anywhere on the planet.

Spiritual law and Jesus' commandment is to Love one another.

When I finally made it back to Florida, I had managed to spend all my money and break all ties to any institution except for one. I was still the Secretary of The Board of Directors at Unity Church of Christianity. In January, I fulfilled my term on the board. Suddenly, to my surprise, a great peace came over me. I asked myself, "How can this be? You have just lost everything." Then it hit me. I had been searching for God in the form of a woman, the form of an allegedly spiritually based institution, in the Village of Harmony and in the church. I had forgotten to look within. I was looking everywhere except where he had always been, right here in my own Heart. I had been looking for God in all the wrong places.

My association with all of these institutions had died and I remembered The Prayer Of Saint Francis Of Assisi, "It is in dying that we are born to eternal life." That, for me meant a dying of the ego. That is what I believe had been happening to me for the previous three years. I finally knew, once again, that I had really gotten what I had been praying for, and that what had seemed like a curse, was in fact a blessing.

Free Agent

In recognition of this new awareness, I entered the following sentiments into my journal on January 10, 1997:

> *While my soul was crying out for freedom my conditioning was drafting me for duty. This week I witnessed it, and today I realized what I had witnessed. I was drawn back to say good-bye to these duties and instead saw them fall away. With the intention of discerning without judging, I believe that while these institutions are intended for providing service to God and mankind, that they are still created in the image of man and chartered in man's world. For me, a separation from that identity and affiliation allows me to be integrated with all that is. It seems that I am being shown that by saying that*

I belong to one group, I am setting an energy field that automatically makes the illusion I am separate from everything else a reality. I have been making that illusion a reality.

This week I returned to the Loren Quinn Institute, to say hello, so I thought. In reality it was to say goodbye. Yesterday, I went to the church board meeting for the last time. This morning, I was relieved but didn't know why. Now I know that it's because I'm free. Now I can join with the church, without joining it. Now I can roam freely calling everyone my family and the Earth my home.

The only organization that I want to belong to is the human race. If I am one with all, with everything in life, I don't have to join an organization to support it. By only joining the human race there is no us or them, so the term "us versus them" has no reference point and therefore disappears.

I had been looking for God in all the wrong places.

This experience as captured in these journal notes has inspired a new way of life for me as a free agent. One day I may become a member of an organization again, but only if it is clear that the purpose of the group is to serve God, not our egos, and that when egos get in the way that the group will consult with head-quarters. "Going to headquarters" was Unity Church co-founder Charles Fillmore's way of say-ing that he would seek his answer through prayer and defer all decisions to God.

Let It Begin With Me

Happy, Healthy, Joyous and Free...
My wish for you,
My wish for me,
And all the members of my Global Family.

Peace on Earth

Christmas Card 1996

Global Family

In the spirit of celebrating the truth that we are all family, I set out to create a proclamation of that, incorporating this blessing; "Happy, healthy, joyous and free; my wish for you, my wish for me and all of the members of my family tree." My little graphics elf, Cat, couldn't come up with a satisfactory rendering that showed the diversity of people all growing from the same tree but the idea came in handy at Christmas time. I changed the words a little and Cat was able to make a fine graphic depiction that turned into our 1996 Christmas card.

By the way, my friend in Santa Fe, Kay Tanaka, contributed the "Happy, healthy, joyous and free" part of the dialogue. (Gee, this really was a family effort, wasn't it?)

The human race is one family and this is my pulpit to spread the gospel of unity. May we all share Martin Luther King's dream that "All of God's children, blacks and whites, Jews and Gentiles, Protestants and Catholics, will be able to join hands and sing in the words of the old Negro spiritual. "Free at last! Free at last! Thank God Almighty, we are free at last!"

The truth is we're family, Children of God are we, And our Holy purpose is to help others to see.

The World Of Spirit

Mother, Mother Ocean

Our beautiful planet is covered by one great ocean. There is no place where it is disconnected/separated and yet we give it different names in different places. Like the great ocean, we are one people, one race, but we give it many separate names. Since the truth is that we are all really one, may we awaken to this truth and may the truth set us free.

Weave, weave, weave us together,
Weave us together in unity and Love.
Weave, weave, weave us together.
Weave us together, together in Love.

Rosemary Crow

The World Of Spirit

The conditions of man have anchored our feet
Have blinded our vision
Have shortened our reach

In the world of spirit only Love abides
It has no conditions; It never derides

Love lifts us and broadens our view of the world
It reveals no limits
And our potential is unfurled

Our feet become springs to launch us into space
Our eyes become windows to the spiritual race
We reach out with our arms
We stretch out our hands
To our brothers and sisters throughout all the lands

Then Love forms a bridge over all that is bleak
From that Bridge we look out and see all that we seek
We're all in this together in this Earthly realm
Spirits in bodies with God at the helm

Those that are aware cannot deny
That to say we are separate is simply a lie
The truth is we're family; Children of God are we
And our Holy purpose is to help others to see

So we go forth with Joy, divinely guided
To fulfill God's promise
All creatures on Earth, Finally United

SOMEWHERE IN KANSAS, WINTER 1994

Why can't we just hug you
and know we are one,
every tree, every human,
the wind, stars and sun

Prayer For The Tree

I wrote the poem "Prayer For The Tree" while sitting beside a mountain stream that was running through a forest of Aspen trees. This site was in a National Forest in Santa Fe, New Mexico, a place I discovered by the most amazing Grace. My friend Mike brought me here to camp during my summer of '96 trip to "The Land Of Enchantment." This particular place lived up to the name.

During this camping trip I would begin each day with a hike that would lead me along the side of one of the two mountain streams that bordered each side of the campground. I felt very connected to the source of life and I felt very alive. As I ventured off of the trails I noticed that I was springing and jumping from place to place. I had awakened the child within me. It occurred to me then that, as a child, climbing and chasing butterflies were great fun. I did not need fancy toys to be happy. Guess what? I still didn't.

But even as I was enjoying this childlike wonder, something was not quite right. As I went to hug another of my Aspen Tree friends I noticed that this one was particularly scarred. It had the initials of the many who had hiked here before me and defaced this beautiful tree with what had now become gross examples of human insensitivity. It must hurt, I thought to myself. I did not quite know what it would be like to be a tree and have my flesh gouged and stripped away, but I was certain that I would feel pain and disrespect. My own pain inspired me to pray that this mindless behavior would stop and that all humans would realize their oneness with the tree, and instead of carving into it, give it a big hug.

It is my belief that all living things are connected and these Aspen trees are one of the great reminders of our unseen connection. Aspens have a common root system, an unseen, underground connection so that what appears to be a forrest of lone trees is actually one grove of trees that makes up the largest living organism in the world.

The Earth does not belong to man,
man belongs to the Earth.

All things are connected like
the blood that unites us all.

Man did not weave the web of life,
he is merely a strand in it. Whatever he
does to the web he does to himself.

CHIEF SEATTLE

৶৶

Get Me Out Of Here, Can't You See I'm Sick

We need healthier hospitals, hospitals that write prescriptions for hugs instead of hospitals that reek with chemical odors and prescribe chemicals for every ailment.

Every Saturday, in the summer of 1997 I would wear the costume of flower delivery guy for Harry's Famous Flowers. It didn't pay a lot of money, but it was something I was happy to be doing each Saturday. As you can imagine, one of the most common stops was at hospitals, delivering kindness and beauty to the patients. My first hospital flower delivery was cold and unfriendly. It triggered a memory from a year or so prior, in which, while visiting a friend in the hospital, a voice inside my head said "Get me out of this place, can't you see I'm sick?" I thought to myself at the time that if you tried to design a place with a less conducive atmosphere for healing, that you'd be hard pressed to do it.

On my first few flower deliveries the experiences were all about the same. I would enter this busy, crowded and hustle/bustle atmosphere where all the people who worked there seemed hassled. If I asked for directions, for instance, they would usually look at

We need healthier hospitals that write prescriptions for hugs.

me with disdain and let me know that giving directions was not their job. The hallways were dark with low ceilings and the hospital rooms were cramped and usually dark as well. Everywhere you went it smelled like sickness and death, not healing and life.

One day I made a delivery to the Arnold Palmer Hospital for Children and Women. This place had an atmosphere that was totally different than all the others. It was full of natural light. So were all the people, staff and patients alike. The pace was slow and the population spread out. Everyone was friendly and helpful and there was a feeling of life everywhere. There were pictures on the walls of living things and paintings of colorful fish. The walls were painted in pastels, not antiseptic white. The place didn't feel at all like sickness and death. It felt like wellness and life.

Then it occurred to me that these surroundings were designed for women and children. The message I was getting was that all the other hospitals just catered to regular sick people, women and children were different. They need beauty and happy things. Of course, those other hospitals also have women and children in them, but they aren't the specific focus. NEWS FLASH: The feminine nature is the nurturing nature and the child nature is the innocent nature. NEWS FLASH: Every human being has a masculine and a feminine side to them and every grown up person still has a child inside of them. We need nurturing when we're sick and we need to recognize the vulnerable child inside everyone, regardless of age or gender, to properly instigate healing.

Our masculine attributes have their place in the healing process but we don't need hospitals that look like army barracks and nurses who act like drill sergeants.

Dr. Rachel Naomi Remen, noted author, Director of the Institute for the Study of Health and Illness and Medical Director of the Commonwealth Cancer Help Retreat Program, makes the following statement in her book *The Eye of an Eagle, The Heart of a Lion, The Hand of Women*: "I'd like to examine the most ancient of human problems–wounding, illness, suffering, and recovery–from a feminine perspective. I'd like to start with a premise. We are all wounded. Everyone has pain. There are only wounded people: We all need healing.

"Our medical system needs healing as well. So here is another part of the premise: Our wounds and the wounds of the medical system are very similar. The reintegration of the feminine principle, the feminine perspective, is a

Every human being has a masculine and a feminine side to them and every grown up person still has a child inside of them.

R_x

12 HUGS DAILY.

REFILLS: 1,000,000,000,000

major step in our own personal healing and the healing of our medical system."[1]

The Arnold Palmer Hospital for Children and Women seems to be a perfect model for the implementation of Dr. Remen's premise and perspective. It's a healthy hospital, but most of them aren't. If I ever get real sick, I'm going to dress in drag and go there.

Oh, by the way, I learned to adjust to the typical hospital by turning up the voltage on my Heart light. In most cases it changed the energy for the better. Even in those places where my Heart light can't penetrate, it's doing a fine job of protecting me from the darkness as I go on smiling and blessing everyone.

Painfully Aware

As I mentioned before, I could only imagine what it feels like to be the tree. If humans really could feel the pain of other people and other life forms we would almost certainly cease to commit such cruel acts.

The movie *Powder* is a powerful story about a teenage boy (his real name is Jamie but he is such a pale white color that they call him Powder) whose incredible brain causes an electrical field around him that attracts things to him like lightning and other electrical currents. Jeff Goldblum played the role of his physics teacher and described Powder as "human electrolysis" because the electrical current that was running through him made it impossible for hair to grow on his body.

Powder was given an IQ test by his high school

and the results showed that he had the highest IQ ever registered. He also had great psychic and intuitive powers and was considered a freak by everyone in the country town where he lived.

In one of the most gripping scenes of any movie that I've ever seen, Powder uses his power to give us a glimpse of what it might be like to really feel the pain of another animal. He is on a camping trip with a group of boys his age when their chaperon, the town deputy, pulls out a rifle and shoots a deer, hitting him in the neck and dropping him in his tracks. While the rest of the group is celebrating the kill, a horrified Powder rushes toward the animal and covers the wound of the dying animal with his hand. The hunter/chaperon walks up right next to him and demands that Powder get away from the animal. Powder jumps up and grabs the man by the throat and, with the other hand, gently grabs the animal's wound. Then, acting as a conductor, he transfers the animal's feelings into the man making him writhe in pain and turn blue. Powder turned loose just before the deer died and just in time to spare the man's life, but not without an emergency trip to the hospital and a couple of days stay there. Needless to say, this man quickly changed his perspective, sold all of

I'm learning to adjust by turning up the voltage on my Heart light.

his guns and vowed to never hunt again.

Powder had a great sense of his connectedness to everything. In fact, he couldn't get away from it. In the end, he was just too sensitive for this world. Every time he saw an act of cruelty against anyone or anything, it ripped his Heart out.

The Placebo Effect

The placebo effect is a well know term, but a poorly understood phenomenon. It is typically associated with the reversal of a medical condition after administering an inert substance to a patient who has been led to believe that he or she has been ingesting the latest pharmaceutical breakthrough. Most people think that this is evidence that the condition and the resulting symptoms never existed; they were all in the person's mind and the belief that the drugs would heal the person tricked them.

The key term here is belief. The person believed that he was sick and usually the symptoms actually manifested in the body. He didn't just perceive himself to be sick, he was. Thoughts create things and in this case the things showed up in the form of disease. Break that down and it becomes dis-ease. The belief that the placebo would make him better caused ease and he got better.

Belief and faith are the same thing. Jesus taught us that all things are possible if we have faith. Few remember that he actually made the statement "Take Heart, daughter; your faith has made you well," taking no direct credit for the healing. It wasn't the touching of Jesus' garment that healed the young girl, it was the belief (faith) that it would.

When was the first time that you experienced the placebo effect? I already know the answer. It was when your mother kissed your boo-boo and made it better. This was a double whammy, first of all, because you believed that your mother's kiss was magic, and secondly, because it really was. Your belief healed you and your mother's Love healed you.

God Bless the placebo effect and God Bless mothers.

Check Your Fluid

This is not presented in the plural because it's not a suggestion that you pop your hood and check your dip sticks before operating your automobile. It is however, an effective metaphor about maintaining optimum running conditions for your physical and emotional vehicle.

Just like our cars we periodically find ourselves sputtering, chugging and missing, without really knowing why. When this happens it's time to check our fluid. Ask yourself the question, am I in the flow of life? The answer may become obvious to you right away, especially if you are caught up in the rushing rapids of modern life that keep pushing you along precariously and throwing you crashing into

The medicine was Love, by far the most potent medicine of all.

the rocks time after time. Or maybe you have become so complacent that your pool of life has begun to stagnate.

Life works really well when we emulate the substance that comprises the majority of our physical being, water. The planet that we inhabit and the bodies that we live in are made primarily of this Divine fluid. Since water is the most non-resistant substance in the world that makes every human being inherently just what they want to be, irresistible!

While it is unnatural for us to be constantly stopping and starting, hurtling forward then throwing on the brakes, that is how society has conditioned us to operate. Stops and starts, beginnings and endings. Then there's the river.

The river represents life. It doesn't struggle to flow, that is its nature. It is also our nature to flow, yet we have forgotten that nature. We have also forgotten that we are all connected to each other like the river is connected to its source.

The thing that we call Grace is flowing movement. The reason that we experience calm when we watch a beautiful dancer in the act of dancing is because the dancer awakens a subconscious memory of our true nature. When we listen to music we are taken to a magical state because the notes flow together and take us to a place that only our hearts can know.

We can perform our own ballet and conduct our own symphony, just by paying attention to the way our own lives are moving. We can find our pace with practice. We can recall our natural rhythm if we are patient.

Next time your life feels out of sync, don't take your temperature, check your fluid.

Sacred Medicine

In the Native American tradition anything that brings about healing or happiness is considered to be good medicine, everything from potions, to prayer, to a sweet smile. In the movie *Dances With Wolves*, Kevin Costner played the part of a soldier who had been dispatched to an abandoned post in the West. He befriended the only people that he had seen for months, the local Sioux Indian tribe.

He initially became acquainted with them when he was out exploring one day. He had rescued a young squaw who was trying to take her life and end her grief for the husband that she had just lost.

When "Dances With Wolves" (Costner's given Indian name) and "Stands With A Fist" fall in Love, she tells no one, but everyone can tell by how happy she is. One day her tribal father looks at her and says, "You and 'Dances With Wolves' make good medicine." The medicine was Love, by far the most potent medicine of all.

The most sacred medicine that I've ever administered and received was

Since water is the most non-resistant substance in the world that makes every human being inherently just what they want to be, irresistible!

when I had the privilege to join with people in prayer from around the world, in the Silent Unity prayer room at Unity Village.

I have first-hand experience with the world's most powerful healing organization. Silent Unity fields well over one million telephone calls each year for one-on-one prayer, with a silent partner, the greatest healer of all, the only true healer, God.

The lines are never closed because God never goes on vacation.

I was a proud member of the Nite-Lights. This wonderful spiritual family prayed with open Hearts with callers in the dark of night, and often during the dark night of their soul. From the time that I would answer the phone with "Silent Unity, how may we pray with you?" until the time that I said goodbye, reminding the person that we would hold them in the collective consciousness of prayer for 30 days, I would plug into their words and feelings while they described their prayer need. Then, before I spoke, I would breathe deeply as I listened for God's voice to speak through me to deliver the right and perfect healing/guiding prayer.

In this place I was able to witness what I considered to be instantaneous healings. On most occasions, when I would say, Amen, I would hear two sounds in succession. The first was a deep sigh of relief and release, the other was a gentle, quiet and Heartfelt, "thank you."

Often the callers would ask me if I could send them the prayer that I had just prayed. I realized that I not only couldn't send it to them, but that I couldn't even repeat it. The prayer that had been prayed was a blessing from God that was delivered for that moment. Its effectiveness had to go beyond the words now and be transformed in their Heart.

Terminally Well

When I worked at Silent Unity I realized that you can feel another person's pain and I also was reminded of the power of Love to transform the pain.

Lately, I have been challenged as I have witnessed many acts of inhumanity that are, for many people, a normal part of everyday life. I'm talking primarily about general inconsideration, gestures of hatred made by hurried drivers on the highway, condescendingly cutting criticism exchanged by people in the work place and many other overt and subtle displays of "me vs. you," or "us vs. them" behavior. Some of these acts are directed right at me. Some are directed at others and I am a detached observer. In the past, my reactions would have varied from a cowering acceptance to a defiant strike-back.

On occasion, I still have a momentary conditioned reflex. However, through my reconditioning process, I am usually guided by spirit and apply spiritual laws to the situation. How I respond is governed by spiritual discernment. Kindness and Love always

Life is permanent. It is death that is temporary.

are the tools that I carry around in my spiritual tool box.

What I am learning is to deepen my compassion, not only for the victims but for the victimizers, because in the end they are only striking out from a place of their own pain and insecurity. It is all a crying out for more Love.

So I pollinate and I know that there will be carriers of the pollen that I leave and that the Love will spread and grow.

If I can feel another person's pain, they can feel my Love. If you can feel another person's pain they can feel your Love. If we realize that we are all in pain, we can all soothe each other with our Love. Then we can heal, individually and collectively.

When we heal, we don't just numb the pain for a little while, we become alive. Life is permanent. It is death that's temporary. Are we going to continue to look at life as hopelessly difficult and painful?

Are we still going to identify patients as terminally ill? If we can go to the Heart of healing, the Heart of Love, we can declare a new decree. When someone asks how you're doing, especially after you've been sick and you're on the mend, answer them with a Loving smile and these words, "I'm Terminally Well, thank you."

Standing at the crossroads,
Trying to read the signs
To tell me which way I should go
To find the answer and all the time I knew,
Plant your Love and let it grow.[2]

ERIC CLAPTON
"Let It Grow"

Prayer For The Tree

How does it feel when they cut into your skin?

Carving their initials for their next of kin
We're all family, that's what I say
One day we'll all know that
That's what I pray
If the carver of the bark was aware of the fact
Surely he wouldn't dare to commit such an act

How does it feel when they cut into your skin?
Leaving scars on your body in a game no one wins
Why can't we just hug you and know we are one
Every tree, every human, the wind, stars and sun

Oh, tree of the forest both great and small
You give beauty to the planet, you give beauty to us all
I pray that whatever it is that you feel
That the carvers will stop and allow you to heal
That your sisters and brothers one day will know
They are safe from all creatures
Those that build nests in your branches
And those that admire your features

How does it feel when they cut into your skin?
Soon it will stop, this is my prayer
That humans will cease committing these sins

And we'll all be one
In the great circle of life
Where everyone wins

SANTA FE, NEW MEXICO, SUMMER 1996

*In thine image
we all are formed,
in truth and love
we are all adorned*

The Essence Of Thee

"The Essence of Thee" was the first poem that I ever put into print. This poem portrayed my perception of God in January of 1994 and, while the other poems add other qualities to Him, Truth and Love remain as the most pure essence. Hence, this poem represents a lasting road map of truth for me.

Freedom is also a very important aspect of God and our relationship with Him. If we can recognize that we are spirits in bodies, then we will always be able to claim our Divine birthright as free beings.

Love is the key we must turn
Truth is the flame we must burn
Freedom the lesson we must learn[1]

LESLEY DUNCAN
"Love Song"

৪৯

The Many Forms Of God

Many people have reported acts of heroism that were performed during a crisis by a "person" who mysteriously showed up on accident scene, saved a life or lives, then just as mysteriously disappeared, never to be seen or heard from again. Often the beneficiary of the heroic act is certain that their savior was an angel. Angels are agents for and aspects of God, they appear in many forms, and bless us in many ways, from simple acts of kindness to profound demonstrations of valor.

In the movie *Oh God*, the role of God is played by George Burns, a man of almost 90 years at the time the movie was made. Lately, God has been appearing to me in a similar form. These are real people. They don't disappear mysteriously but they are no less agents of God than the angels described above.

Built To Last

On one particular occasion in the winter of 1996, I met with God at the seashore. Since that's the place where I feel most connected with God any-way, I guess it should come as no surprise. On this day, I was particularly concerned with answering the question "what's next?" That is, what's the next step after I leave this body? So I gazed upon the water in quiet contemplation while casting the question to the winds. I wasn't really expecting a direct answer anytime soon, but for some reason reincarnation was rolling around in mind almost to the point of annoyance.

After a while, I was ready to go for my customary walk, a brisk one for exercise. Because my purpose is to exercise, I don't usually stop for any reason. When I'm in a space like this, I'm not normally interested in having conversation with anyone.

So I'm walking along, minding my own business, when this tall, elderly man starts walking toward me, talking animatedly about a sea gull with one leg. At first, I'm hardly listening to this old guy with a Swedish accent. I'm only pretending to pay attention. Suddenly something kicks in, I stop pretending and I start to pay attention for real. The old man was lamenting about an acquaintance of his, a one legged, one winged bird. A tragedy of nature, he said. He was holding a piece of bread in his hand, I noticed, as he described how it was unfair for the small birds to have to fight the big birds for food. They had no chance, he explained. Then he divulged his true purpose. He wanted to "change the system." He would feed the little birds and make the big ones fend for themselves.

Angels are agents for and aspects of God.

Another thing that I noticed about this gentleman was his hat. It was kind of a sailors cap with a button on it that said "Built To Last." I pointed to the button and reading aloud said, "built to last." The old man smiled broadly and said "I'm 84 years old. I get to do this for 16 more years, then I get to come back and start all over again. That's just the way it is." We both smiled again and walked our separate ways.

This man answered the question that I had posed to the Universe just moments before. Was this a coincidence? Only to the biggest skeptics, I think. It was a profound demonstration to me and one of the quickest responses I'd ever gotten. "Built To Last" was a messenger from God, an Angel, or maybe just plain God.

Bobby

One day in the fall of 1996, after not playing golf for months, I went to the municipal golf course in the Orlando suburb of Winter Park to "tee it up." This is a place where you can play very inexpensively and you are allowed to walk. Most golf courses today require you to rent a golf cart to ride around in while chasing that little white dimpled ball.

Since I hadn't played in a while, I was really hoping that I could escape alone without a playing partner. I paid my greens fees and while standing on the tee alone loosening up, I noticed an old man out in the parking lot. This guy looked real old and he was so slouched over that his nose was pointing toward the ground. I thought to myself, "this guy's not going to mess with a young whipper snapper like me. I'll be off by myself in just a minute. "

After swinging the club a couple of more times something caused me to turn my head and watch this guy spryly truckin' across the parking lot, golf clubs in tow. A feeling came over me and I thought to myself, "what a beautiful human being." This had to be the first time in my life that I had described an old hunched-back man as beautiful. I must have been taken by his determination to play in spite of his condition.

Just when I was about to tee off I heard a voice. I turned and there he was, the old hunched-back man grinning a grin the size of Texas. He wanted to know if I was looking for a playing partner. Well of course I wasn't, but I said "sure" anyway, which was a noncommittal way for me to sidestep my real feelings and spare his.

The old man stepped forward, extended his hand and said "I'm Bobby," the grin even more prominent now. I introduced myself in the same first-name-only manner. He seemed genuine as he stated that it was his pleasure to meet me.

Bobby was old in years, weathered by time and full of battle scars, but this man had learned the secrets to a good life. He had no insecurities about who he was. He was fearless and he was happy. And he hit the ball down the middle of the fairway while I was spraying the ball in every direction.

From the very beginning, this Southern gentleman was complimentary. When I hit my ball into a beautiful estate across the road from the first hole, he told me that I had a nice swing and that I just needed to straighten it out a bit. He offered to retrieve the ball for me so that I could play my provisional ball. It was all the way on the

The old saying to "count your blessings" isn't just a cute saying, it is an empowering exercise.

other side of the fairway. As I tracked my second ball down and prepared to hit, I looked across and saw Bobby looking high and low for my first ball, even looking in the bushes of the manicured estate that he was trespassing in. He was going to much more trouble than I would have to find my own golf ball, let alone somebody else's.

By now I had become quite amazed by this man. When we met back up again in the fairway, I just had to ask the question, "What keeps you smiling, Bobby?" Bobby grinned that grin and said "I'm just glad to be here. I'm 81 years old. I've been through three wars, had both of my knees replaced and numerous other operations, but I have a good life. I've been married to the same woman for (umpteen) years and I get to play golf three days a week. I couldn't ask for more."

Bobby had latched on to one of the most powerful and important spiritual principles. The old saying to "count your blessings" isn't just a cute saying, it is an empowering exercise.

Bobby was obviously a master at it and, as I learned in the two and half hours that I spent with him, many other important things. He was a generous man. Not only was he generous with compliments to me, finding things to praise me for in the midst of what I considered to be considerable ineptitude, but he hardly could contain his excitement about the afternoon he had planned. He was going to surprise his wife and take her car shopping. He just couldn't wait to buy her a spanking new car.

We finished our round of golf. As we were saying goodbye, I told him that it had been an honor to play with him and that I was particularly inspired by his appreciation of life. He thanked me and told me that he had always been that way, even during the "Great Depression." Then he gave me one last pearl of wisdom. The good old days weren't really better, he said. I think that he was telling me to count my blessings and be here now.

I was right. Bobby was a beautiful human being, and much more. I had a Tee Time with God this day and I almost canceled it.

Grace prevailed, and to my good fortune, I kept the appointment and walked away with treasures that are laid up in Heaven, inside my Heart.

It takes two hands to make a friend.

Juan and Two

I Love making new friends that I just meet along the way. I made a new friend today and learned something new from her. I started the conversation by reading the front of her shirt. It said "It takes two hands to make a friend." This hearing-impaired person showed me the "sign" for friend. It is done by interlocking the index fingers on your right and left hand. If you're close friends you lock your fingers and pull them tightly together. This former stranger honored me by telling me that we were close friends then demonstrating the exercise for me.

June doesn't even know my name but I'm tight with her. She used to rent me videos at the grocery store, but now she's in another department. Wherever June is, though, she's spreading light and Love. I've never seen her when she wasn't smiling, laughing or trying to make you laugh. She's what my mother would have called "a pistol." I'm not sure just what her chronological age is but I'm pretty sure that this child at Heart was a Depression Era baby.

On the other hand, I know exactly how old Juan is. He turned 72 on June 26. The reason that I know this is because on the morning of June 13 he told me that it was time for him to "start celebrating because I have a birthday coming up." He conveyed this to me while I was warming up for my daily walk/workout at one of my favorite places to do that, Cranes Roost Park, a few miles north of Downtown Orlando. Just as I was beginning to stretch my legs on the bars that have been so conveniently placed there, a short jolly Hispanic man walked right up to me and started talking. He told me about his birthday, how young he felt and how he taught school in Brooklyn for 45 years. He also told me that he had a brother named Tu (He didn't spell it for me). So that people could remember, he explained, he would say, "I'm Juan and he's Tu" (Two). Juan was vitally alive even though he was 70–Juan getting ready to turn 72. Another blessing, another aspect of God in the flesh.

The Champ

On the evening of November 9, 1996, Evander Holyfield entered the boxing ring a 12 to 1 underdog in the Heavyweight Championship fight against Mike Tyson, the man carrying the title of heavyweight champ going into the fight. The prevailing opinion was not only that Tyson would win but that he would punish Holyfield severely. What really happened was that the referee stopped the fight in the eleventh round and declared Evander Holyfield the winner and new heavyweight champion by technical knockout.

Love has no limits, so just set it free.

Everyone was certain that Holyfield would lose but Holyfield. In all the pre-fight interviews, he had said that God would give him the strength to win. This drew many snide attempts at humor from the Tyson camp, including Tyson's comment, "what am I going to do when I knock him down, throw holy water on him?" He never had the chance to find out. It was he that got knocked down.

Heart Full Of Love

When Evander Holyfield entered the ring that night, he had the following inscription on his boxing trunks, "It is the Christ within that strengthens me." In the true spirit of the Christ, he never took the credit. He always gave the glory to God.

You may be wondering how I can glorify a brutal sport like boxing. It can be brutal. But that is what Evander Holyfield was born to do and the boxing ring is his pulpit and a way for him to glorify God to millions of people.

In another one of those Divine coincidences, I got to meet the man one night while wearing my chauffeur costume. I was driving his children and baby sitter around while he rode in the car in front of me. I explained to his young daughters and their adult chaperon that I was writing a book and that I was going to write about their father. I also asked them if they would like for me to recite a poem for them and they said yes. I recited this poem, "The Essence of Thee." They all clapped. A little while later, one of the girls innocently asked me if I could tell them another poem. So I recited "Heart Full of Love," and they clapped again. Their sweet energy was a great blessing.

When we dropped them all off at the movies, I got my first chance to meet "The Champ." He graciously autographed a note pad for me with the following "Holyfield Phil 4:13." He was referencing the Bible passage in the fourth chapter of Philippians. In my Revised Standard Version of the Holy Bible the passage reads, "I can do all things in Him who strengthens me."

Evander Holyfield knows his Bible well and he also knows the source of his strength. Just like when Jesus said "Why do you call me good? It is not I but the Father who does his great work through me." Evander Holyfield is a living example of Jesus' word. Even his signature identifies the real champ.

The Mouths Of Babes

Recently I traded out some house painting for some healing work with my friend Kim. (I did the painting, she did the healing).

It took me a few trips to the house to complete the project because I was only able to work a couple of hours at a time.

On my first trip, I brought three Mardi Gras bead necklaces as a house gift. They quickly became the property of Kim's three year old daughter Brigitte, and we became fast friends.

One day when I went to paint, I was particularly aware of my nerdy appearance. I had on an ugly painter's hat, studious looking glasses, a muscle shirt for my not so muscular arms and a myriad of contrasting colors in my wardrobe. It mattered not to Brigitte. She was very excited to see me as she followed me around calling my name and showing off with somersaults while her daddy held her arms and she swung herself around. She also had other tricks including swinging herself on the swing set, belly down.

Brigitte was demonstrating pure unconditional Love and I was delighted. You see, she hadn't learned what a nerd was yet and all she saw was someone who Loved her by paying attention to her.

I can do all things in Him who strengthens me.

Let It Shine

God comes to me in many forms. In fact, God is everywhere. It's just that he's harder to see in some places than in others.

For me the strongest presence of God's qualities, as defined in my poem, come from the very old and the very young. Perhaps it is because they are both naturally closer to him than the rest of us. The reason that I use the term "naturally" is because babies just came from God and they haven't yet forgotten their true nature. It hasn't yet been covered over with the illusory veil of society's conditioning. The older folks are getting closer to home and perhaps they're starting to remember what it's like there. Perhaps they're just wiser. After all that's what's supposed to happen when you get older.

Those of us in the middle are no less children of God than the folks on each end, but our light doesn't shine as brightly as most of theirs do. It's time we started looking to them to remind us of who we really are. When we do, our lights will shine brighter and the more we shine, the more the people that are around us will shine and the essence of God will appear everywhere we look.

The Two Faces Of God

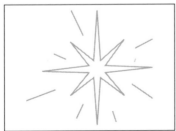

The Essence Of Thee

All thoughts that come which do not embrace
The essence of God's good Grace

I shall cast aside and let fade away

Into nothingness
And that's where they'll stay

For Truth is Truth
And Love is Love

God is both
That much I'm certain of

Shout it from the Heavens on high
Then look deep inside to
Where the greatest treasures lie

For in Thine image we all are formed

In Truth and Love we are all adorned

So let us be what we truly are
A radiant being
A shining star

Let us shine our light
For all to see

Truth and Love
The Essence of Thee

LAKE IVANHOE, ORLANDO, FLORIDA, WINTER 1994

There are oceans in us all
and much more you see
because a part of the
creator's inside you and me

The Presence Of The Power

While the previous poem talks about God in his many forms, "The Presence of the Power" is about aligning ourselves with that power. That was what Jesus did and that's what he was teaching us to do.

We can align ourselves with God's power in many ways as we abide by spiritual laws and put the power of intention to work through prayer. All our thoughts are prayers and those prayers are all answered in some form or fashion.

Up until a few years ago, I thought that I had bad luck. I was a victim of a fate that I couldn't control. That was what I believed and that's the way things worked out for me. When I would first get to know people, I would tell them that I had bad luck and they would usually tell me that they didn't believe in such a thing. After they hung around with me for a while they'd change their minds. Eventually they would say, you're right, you do have bad luck.

Later on in life, after I'd changed my way of thinking, I began to draw good things into my world and people began to comment on my good fortune.

Now and then I fall back into the old thought patterns and forget my Divine heritage. My thoughts sometimes revert to tribal limitation thoughts and I'll sometimes find myself having "bad luck" again.

Through mindfulness this reversion can be largely averted, and even when it's not we can quickly convert back to our spiritual awareness. Breathe and follow this formula and you'll get back on the right track: Follow spiritual laws, Love your neighbor and pray in gratitude giving thanks for already receiving your good. In time, you will get what you want or something greater.

This chapter is about the power of intention, synchronicity, manifestation, and other examples of Divine Intervention. It will address co-creation, creating a life in partnership with God. You will see many examples of magical, wonderful and Divine events as they have occurred in my life. Some of them may seem minor to you and some major. Either way, they are all true.

In time you will move mountains,
It will come through your hands.[1]

JOHN HIATT
"Through Your Hands"

ℰℛ

The Power Of Intention

Intention, in the spiritual sense, is when you act upon something with a specific intention in mind and Heart. It also may be known as living on purpose. Either way, when you are living according to spiritual law, your intentions are always good. From this perspective, the saying, "the road to Hell is paved with good intentions," is a statement that is invalid and born out of ignorance. There is a card taped to the mirror in my bathroom that expresses that notion with these words, "No one fails who does their best for God."

There is great power in intention especially when that intention is being shared by a collective effort to raise the consciousness for good and honorable aims. That is one of the main reasons that Silent Unity is so effective. Your prayer is held in the consciousness of all the prayer room workers, 24 hours a day for 30 days in a special prayer vigil room.

Jesus taught us about the power of collective prayer and intention when he said "For where two or three are gathered in my name, there I am in the midst of them."

I have seen Carlos Santana and his band more than any other musician(s). I've lost count of the number of times,

No one fails who does their best for God.

but it's around nine or 10. During one of the recent incredible concert experiences, Carlos witnessed to the potent power of intention.

As is characteristic of this great man, he paused between songs and stepped to the front of the stage with his hands clasped and his face pointed toward the Heavens. Slowly, as if waiting for God's words to come, he spoke, saying, "We are all powerful and what we think and what we intend makes a difference.

"When we join in our intentions we see mighty things happen. In 1989, we played in Berlin and we proclaimed that this wall must come down. In less than one year it was down. We went to south Africa to play there and said, this man Mandela must be freed, and now he is their President."

These are profound examples of the immense power of intention. This is a power that is available to us all individually. When we join together in our intentions, the power grows exponentially.

Synchronicity Strikes Again

The basic definition of synchronicity is Divine coincidence. It isn't necessary for two or more people to share the experience but that's often the case. This aspect of the phenomenon occurs when people have exactly the same thoughts, dreams, or ideas, for no apparent reason, at exactly the same time, even though they may be miles apart. The most common occurrence of synchronicity is probably when two people who haven't talked to each other in months pick up the telephone at the same time to call each other. I'm not aware of anyone who has not experienced this before.

I think that these "coincidences" happen in large and small ways because there is a cosmic intelligence that is always there, but we are more or less in touch with it depending on our particular attention to this vibrational frequency. Our ability to receive the channel is governed by natural laws, the same laws that are used by our technologies to deliver a clear picture to our television or a clear voice over the telephone. For human beings, we already have the right equipment to receive the transmissions, but most of us don't know how to use it. In fact, there is usually so much interference from the internal and external stimuli that constantly bombards us from all directions, that we couldn't hear the voice of Universal Intelligence, God, if he was using a megaphone. Since it's best to listen for the whisper, most of us are way off.

We already have the right equipment to receive but most of us don't know how to use it.

One example of synchronicity, for me, relates to a series of events that took place for me right after I wrote the poem "Welcome Home." I finally completed the poem in August of 1994. Up until this time, I had never read or heard anything by Marianne Williamson. The day after I finished the poem, I began reading her book, *A Return To Love,* to familiarize myself with her prior to seeing her speak. I already had tickets to see her so I figured I ought to get to know her a little.

After reading the book, I was an instant fan of hers and realized that there was material in her book that addressed the same issues that I had tried to condense into a poem. The night of the concert I decided to give her that poem. So I tucked it under my arm and took it into the auditorium. After an awesome experience of her dynamic presence, I was disappointed to find out that she wasn't going to be available in any way to the general audience, only to a select group at a private affair in another building.

On the way out of the auditorium, we ran into a friend from church. I shared the poem with her and she liked it so much I gave it to her.

Before we got back to the car, I discovered where Marianne was going to be and I sneaked in. Unfortunately, I no longer had "Welcome Home," the poem I had intended to give her, so I gave her the poem "World of Spirit" instead.

A few months later, she was in Kansas City debuting her new prayer book, *Illuminata.* In that book, there was a short, but very exact passage, with the basic theme of my poem "Welcome Home." Did I actually give the poem to her that night, on a cosmic level, or did she send the information to me over the cosmic airwaves, so that I could write the poem to begin with? Synchronicity strikes again.

Tales Of Magic And Wonder
I Am Forrest Gump

Recently the Nike shoe corporation has been showing a commercial in which all of the participants are kids, all different ages, races and genders. When the camera flashes on a kid, each one says "I am Tiger Woods." The commercial's objective is to demonstrate that, regardless of race, creed or gender, all children have the potential within them to be great. They are all Tiger Woods, the young golf phenomenon who defied racial barriers to become the world's best golfer.

We couldn't hear the voice of God, if he was using a megaphone.

One day it occurred to me that I was more like Forrest Gump. The movie character Forrest Gump, from the movie of the same name, was a simple man who made simple gestures, and spoke in simple terms and great things happened around him. While my experiences aren't quite as remarkable as Forrest's, I think there are similarities.

Nick Of Time

It first hit me that day that the Magic played so bravely in defeat to the Miami Heat.

During the game's fourth quarter, after the Magic had fallen quite a few points behind, I had a flash of intuition that said "It's time for Nick Anderson to step up." Nick had been doing nothing but falling down all season so it would have seemed very unlikely that he would step up. I went on about how Nick used to be the "money man" a few years back, the guy who always made the big shots under pressure. I boldly stated that it was his time to regain his form. Within about 60 seconds of actual time (not to be confused with game time) Nick made the first of three 3-point shots leading a Magic comeback, from 16 points behind, to only three. While the Magic fell a little short, Nick's performance was a miracle. I'm pretty sure that I could have gotten 100 to 1 betting odds against this happening.

That night the movie *Forrest Gump* was on TV and I watched it. The next day the sports section of *The Orlando Sentinel* carried this article. "Anderson steps up in the nick of time. Nick Anderson came alive in the fourth quarter and almost rescued the Magic, and his season."

Win One For The King

In March of every year, I attend the local PGA tour stop at Bay Hill. Arnold Palmer is the host of this golf tournament that is played just outside of Orlando. In 1997, I had a season pass which meant that I could go out there every day if I wanted to. The tournament runs four days, starting on Thursday and ending on Sunday.

On Tuesday preceding the real tournament there's a pro-am, an event in which amateur golfers pay a fee and get to play with the pros. Since the pros are doing it just for fun and practice, it's an excellent time to get autographs. I got as many as I could. In each case, I tried to connect with the "person behind the golfer" with some comment that invited feedback. I considered this to be a way to get to know them.

Some of the golfers were really friendly and some couldn't be bothered. On this particular day, I decided that Mark O'Meara was the friendliest guy of all. He signed his autograph, answered my question and acted like we were old friends. Right away I decided that I was going to root for my new friend, Mark O'Meara.

I stayed at the tournament all day on Friday. By the end of the day O'Meara was close to the lead and I was happy. After seeing all the golf I could see in one day, I headed off on the long walk back to my car with only my newly purchased program in hand.

All of a sudden, I saw Phil Mickelson walking off the practice green with no one else around, just me and Phil. I started scrambling for something for him to put his autograph on. The only thing I had was my program, so I quickly found Mickelson's photo in the program and thrust it in front of him for an autograph. With a grin the size of California, (that's where he lives) Phil signed his picture. Phil wasn't real close to the lead at the time, but I decided to ask him how he was feeling,

Be thankful for Love and become awakened to this moment.

you know like, "How's your game?" He looked at me and grinned again saying, "pretty good, how about yourself?" I didn't think it was possible, but he actually seemed even friendlier than O'Meara. Now I was pulling for the long shot, Mickelson, not only because he was at least tied for the nicest golfer award, but because if he won, his would be the only autograph in my program.

What a beautiful story. Mickelson got hot, won the tournament and I coincidentally walked up the eighteenth fairway with his Dad. His Dad was a friendly and talkative guy himself and was pleased to hear that I thought that his son was such a warm and genuine guy. He also said something to the effect that most people think it's an act, that nobody could be that friendly.

At the awards ceremony, Phil was introduced for the first time in public as a married man. His blushing bride joined him on the green.

In his awards acceptance speech, he credited his victory to the inspiration that he had gained while looking at pictures of "The King," Arnold Palmer. Arnie had a flair about him that could be captured in a photograph, as he charged his way from behind to win many golf tournaments.

A storybook ending, as the nicest guy in town, "Won one for the King," and sailed off into the sunset with his bride by his side.

We Have To Stop Meeting Like This

In January of 1994, a couple of friends and I got tickets to see James Redfield, the author of the *Celestine Prophecy,* when he spoke at the Unity

Church in Sarasota, over on Florida's beautiful Gulf Coast.

We stayed overnight on Saturday in a condo a block off the beach on Anna Maria Island, 35 minutes north of Sarasota. On Sunday, we were running late for Redfield's afternoon talk. I was a little anxious on the way over there, thinking that we would have seats so far away by the time we got there that we wouldn't know whether it was James on stage, or an imposter.

Fortunately, my friend Jim had other ideas. He proclaimed that we would end up with seats right in front of the stage. He was on the right track but things ended up being even better than that. The place was so packed that they actually had to set up seats on the stage and we arrived just as they were seating people there. My seat was in the front row on the same level as James R. and only about 10 to 12 feet from the microphone.

It was a great place to watch from and feel James' energy but things got even better at the intermission. There was a line about a mile long going into the bathroom and I was at the end of it, for about 30 seconds. I was standing in this long line when a door opened and I recognized the minister motioning to me to come towards him. He told me that I could use his bathroom as soon

A storybook ending, as the nicest guy in town, "Won one for the King," and sailed off into the sunset with his bride by his side.

as James was done. Duh, I didn't realize that he was talking about the guest of honor. The bathroom door opens and there's James Redfield with a grin the size of Alabama (you guessed it). As we passed in the john, we shook hands, and once again I was amazed at my good fortune.

I feel that this story resembles the Forrest Gump scene in which he is being honored at the White House by President Kennedy for making the college football All American team. While he is waiting for the president, Forrest is filling up on his favorite beverage, Dr. Pepper. When it's his turn to meet the president, the scene shows him waiting in line with his legs crossed and his hand holding his crotch. When he gets up to the president, President Kennedy asks him how it feels, (presumably to be an All American) and Forrest answers "I have to pee." In my case, both James and I had to pee.

What's Your Maiden Name?

My mother died on April 30, 1985, after liver cancer had taken all the life out of her. She was expected to die a few days earlier than she did as she was comatose and said to be brain dead.

During her last few days, she was left in a room by herself to die. I would visit her and just sit with her alone. One night, I was accompanied by a former girlfriend, Sherry. That night she sat with me and we chatted quietly until suddenly my mother spoke the first words that she had spoken in over a week. "Sherry, what's your maiden name?" she inquired.

You see, my mother was a notary and since notaries can marry people in Florida, she was able to create a nice business for herself performing wedding ceremonies for couples. The wedding that she most wanted to attend was mine, and up to this point, it just wasn't to be. Until now. After Sherry answered her, my mother continued. She performed a good portion of the ceremony and, while we didn't quite get to the "I do" part, she had made her point, her final wish. The next morning she made her transition.

The Law Of Least Effort

Deepak Chopra's fourth spiritual law of success is the Law of Least Effort. "This law is based on the fact that nature functions with effortless ease and abandoned carefreeness. This is the principle of least action, of no resistance."[2]

On May 2, 1994, I experienced the most major demonstration of this law, before or since. This day was the coldest day on record in Hot Springs, Arkansas, and it was rainy to boot. But this was the day that Mike and I would go crystal digging.

After being there for a few days and trying to wait out the weather, I could wait no longer. During those few days, we had met with many folks whose commentary on crystal digging left me with low expectations that we would

Nature functions with effortless ease and abandoned carefreeness.

Deepak Chopra

find many crystal treasures. In the first 30 minutes of digging, those expectations had been lived up to. I hadn't found even one crystal. Mike and I were following a technique that was prescribed by some experienced crystal diggers who had invited us to join them in their pile of clay. The method for finding crystals, they said, was to find the gooiest clay and keep breaking into it until you find a crystal. After 30 minutes of practice, I couldn't take it anymore.

Frustrated, I walked over to a dry sandy pile of clay and swatted the top of the hill, only to see a crystal pop out. I called Mike over and we started basically sifting sand and finding crystals left and right. Not many big ones but lots of little shiny ones. Before long we had our bucket pretty full. Since Mike wasn't as well equipped for the rain as I was, he decided to call it a day, and went to the car giving me his blessing to keep on looking.

Attired in the Army issue rain parka that I had picked up at a garage sale for 25 cents, I ventured out away from our pile and started walking around the crystal mine. In no time, I was picking crystals up that were sticking right out of the ground. I'd pick up a handful and walk back to the car, deposit them in the bucket and go right back out again. Each time, I would pass a front end loader that was used to push clay around the digging area. It finally occurred to me to take a closer look. Sure enough, the shovel face of the front end loader had crystals sticking right out of it. I didn't even have to bend down any more. In fact, the biggest and best prize of the day was right there in the front end loader. The point had been made. I was prosperous and I left shortly after this find as a voice inside my head was saying "Don't be greedy."

The harder I tried, the more I repelled. The more that I surrendered, the more I attracted. This spiritual law is dramatically different from tribal laws, but it works a lot better.

Please Pass The Fries

One summer day at Unity Village, I was meditating in a lovely spot in the woods, by a place that I call the cave, when the poem "Heart Full Of Love" came to me. After I had finished my meditation with the poem composed in my head, I made the descent to the floor of this open cavern and looked down toward my feet. The floor of the cave was made of rocks of all sizes. It seemed like every rock was shaped like a Heart. I picked up a few especially good ones and walked back to my car where I sat down to write my poem.

Everywhere I went for the next couple of weeks, I kept finding objects that were shaped like Hearts. Of course, I was sharing my poem and giving away many Heart-shaped objects. If you didn't get one, you at least got the story. Hearts were manifesting, that was clear to me, but you need a big demonstration to convince skeptics. Four of us were treated to the most profound example of manifestation that I'd ever seen.

We are connected to the Source and supplied with the power to create our own dreams hour after hour.

Presence Of The Power

It happened one Sunday night after we had attended a church service in Kansas City. Shirley and Steve in the back seat, Cathy and Jeff (me) in the front. The four of us were riding back from K.C. on the way to a restaurant having a discussion on gun control. I was in favor of it, but Shirley said that it was irrelevant, that we just needed to Love each other and we wouldn't kill each other. At that point I was still in favor of gun control, but I went along with her and proceeded to recite my poem, "Heart Full Of Love."

When we got seated at the restaurant and ordered our food, I had a strange craving for french fries, something I never eat. Shirley agreed to split them with me, so we placed an order to share. When it arrived, there was a huge plate of thin fries, all except for one. The lone exception was flat and shaped perfectly like a Heart. The four of us witnessed this anomaly with mouths agape. We pointed it out to the waitress and she apologized, saying that she'd never seen anything like it before.

Worthless No More

Earlier I told you that my brother had labeled me with the nickname "Worthless" as a child and even though it made my life hard for many years, it has ended up being a blessing.

Dan and I still don't see much of each other, so one day in July of 1997 while I was journaling I stated my intention to get together with my brother for a beer. At that time I would tell him about the debilitating blessing and thank him for it. As I was writing the words "the most debilitating incident of my life was being...What I was intending to write were the words "tagged Worthless" but halfway through the word "tagged" my pen ran out of ink. No matter how hard I pressed I could not make the word worthless appear on the page. The label was gone, disappeared. The spell had been broken. This was an example of reverse manifestation.

Home Sweet Home

Back in the spring of 1994, I was weighing the decision between two choices: 1) Go to Unity Village to live in a spiritual community, work there and be in a romantic relationship, or 2) Take the money that I had saved, buy a computer and find a place that was both close to the beach and to a library. The intention was that I would become immersed in nature and in my writing. I chose the first option and it turned out to be a long and difficult journey, but I grew from it and there-fore, like the debilitating blessing, I am thankful for all it has taught me.

It has been just over three years now since I made that decision and I'm sitting here writing in an atmosphere very similar to the one that I had envisioned as my second option. I'm not as close to the ocean or the gulf as I had hoped for then, but I am closer to water than I thought I would be and I'm walking distance to the library. Right

Love can not be far behind a grateful heart and thankful mind.[3]
A Course In Miracles

now, I'm looking at a small lake that is about 100 feet away and there are so many other bonuses that are above and beyond my dreams. The most magical blend of natural beauty and real life conveniences are just a few steps away. I can walk to the bank, the park, the dry cleaner, the movie theater, and even the golf course or I can just walk out my door and down to the swimming pool. From the pool, I can look out at the second lake while taking a dip. If I had made a list for God, it would have never been this complete and I could never have positioned everything so well.

I now have a most Heavenly atmosphere with a Heavenly attitude, an attitude of utmost gratitude.

The Activating Ingredients

Since this chapter is about magic, miracles and spiritual empowerment, I would be remiss not to give some kind of a formula for this. If you were to boil it all down to the most essential components, or activating ingredients for activating our spiritual power, they would be: *Forgiveness and Gratitude.*

Forgiveness releases the entanglements that hold us in the past and gratitude allows us to join with the goodness that propels us forward.

Be thankful for Love and become awakened to this moment, release any thoughts of error or fault, forgive them, let the past fall away, and you will start the trip back home.

I've been trying to get down to the Heart of the matter... I think it's about forgiveness.[4]

DON HENLEY, J.D. SOUTHER, DANNY KORTMAR
"The Heart of the Matter"

The Presence Of The Power

As awesome as the ocean seems
It's a small manifestation of the
Creator's holy dreams
There are oceans in us all
And much more you see
Because a part of the
Creator's inside you and me

We are connected to the
Source and supplied with the power
To create our own dreams
Hour after hour

As we align with the source of
Beauty, Love and grace
We see His holy presence on
Each and every face
We see it in the birds as
They soar high over the land
We see it in the waves as they pound into the sand
We see it in the dew that
Forms on blades of grass
In the beauty of a sunset as
Another day comes to pass

Then a new day's created,
They're connected to each other
Just as we're connected, my sister and my brother
So feel that awesome presence and know that we are one
With the Creator of it all, whose will is surely being done.

CRANES ROOST PARK, ALTAMONTE SPRINGS, FLORIDA, SPRING 1995

We'll re-write the laws
that say we can't fly,
unpin our wings and
sail into the sky

Welcome Home

*We are meant to ascend,
to transmute the
negative thought forms.
No one asked us to stay so long,
away from Heaven, away from joy.
We needn't wait.
We can go home now.*[1]

MARIANNE WILLIAMSON
Illuminata

᪥

What separates "Welcome Home" from all the other poems is the way in which it was formed. Almost all of my other poems decided to write themselves right away. They were usually completed within an hour or two, from the first seed thought, to the last word. This poem is based upon life circumstances that had bothered me for years and had particularly haunted my thoughts for two or three months prior to the time I exorcised them by putting them in writing.

This poem is about losing our connection to God through a conditioning process that made us forget our true nature. In this conditioning process, we were taught about many illusions that took us away from truth, innocence, joy and Love.

We were conditioned to falsely believe in separation and limitation. Why were we taught these painful untruths? If we had never been exposed to them, we would have never left home in the first place. We would never have forgotten God and we wouldn't have had to get reacquainted. We could be home right now.

But we were led astray. Now the task is to find our way back. This poem challenges us to undo our conditioning and re-write the laws that say we can't fly.

The poems, stories and chapters in this book have an evolutionary order to them that is intended to retrain and restore our memory of who we truly are, so we can remember our Divine heritage.

Truly, we do not need more of anything. We simply need to recognize our abundance and our magnificence, and bring them into full expression.

In the final analysis, we need to become as little children and return to our natural state as bundles of joy.

The little ones are here to teach us how to do that now. They'll teach us how to recover the innocence and return to that natural state.

People who refer to their babies as angels don't realize that they are speaking a powerful truth. The word angel means messenger. Our babies are the messengers who are carrying the message to make us remember and to take us home and God is just waiting for that great day when he can say,

"Welcome home my bundles of joy."

· · · ⊗ · · ·

*Unless you change and
become like little children,
you will never enter the
kingdom of Heaven.*

JESUS CHRIST

*We simply
need to
recognize our
abundance
and our
magnificence,
and bring
them into
full expression.*

Road Map Home

Love Yourself
Love Your Neighbor
Love The Earth
And The World Will Be Full Of Love

Welcome Home

We're born into this world a bundle of joy
We cry out for Love, they hand us a toy
We say, this is nice but its Heart doesn't beat
Can I just have a hug, that would be such a treat

When we get a little bigger we get another toy
And little by little we forget about joy
We begin to believe it's these toys that are real
More and more we forget how it is just to feel

Now we're grown up and we're a bundle of nerves
We dodge all the bullets and swerve through the curves
We've come to believe the world's a dangerous place
But we manage survival at a furious pace

Things are what's real so we keep getting more
Then one day we wake up and say what's this all for

A new day is dawning and it's our job to teach
That Love, joy and peace are all within reach

Dispelling illusions, unlearning untruths
Recovering innocence lost in our youth
Returning to joy, our natural state
Where Love is the power that casts out all hate

The next generation born into this world
Each and every boy, each and every girl
They'll be the teachers, they'll tell us what's real
That Love, joy and peace are the right things to feel

We'll re-write the laws that say we can't fly
Unpin our wings and sail into the sky
We'll stop hoarding possessions, we'll care for each other
Good stewards of the planet, we'll respect our Earth Mother

Yes, we are all God's children and on this great day
He'll look down upon us and this he will say
Welcome home, welcome back, my bundles of joy

CANAVERAL NATIONAL SEASHORE, FLORIDA, SUMMER 1994

*This book is dedicated
to all Mothers everywhere,
but "mine the most of all"*

Everybody's Mother
But Mine The Most Of All

Ball games and birthdays, things you never forgot
Remembering others, something you did quite alot

You were everybody's mother, but mine the most of all
You brought me into this world and I began to crawl
And when I tried to walk you'd catch me when I'd fall
You taught me how to walk, how to talk, then how to run
Even through the toughest times, you always tried to keep things fun

Every event was special, they were all a party to you
The same applied to people, every person special too

You kept the Christ in Christmas and
Filled the house with Heavenly sounds
While cookies were left for baking and presents were being bound
When it came time for turkey everyone was there
Even the sailors from the base with the crew cut hair

Not a birthday came and went when you didn't bake
A cake that was my favorite, my very own special cake

Mom, you set the example of the highest standards yet
If they gave out records for Moms
Yours could never be broken, no never even met.

You set records for giving but you did even more
Honesty and truth were the big things you lived for

You taught me not to judge by the color of one's skin
That there's goodness in us all, and really, we're all kin

You stood up for what was good, you stood up for what was right
You stood up against their enemies, without the slightest bit of fright

You stood up for those among us who couldn't stand up for themselves
You figured someone had to do it, you couldn't wait for someone else

Mom, you were the greatest mother and still are to this day
And I'm the lucky son who has this truth to say

You were everybody's mother, but mine the most of all

MY TRIBUTE TO MOM, EILEEN TRESSLER, WRITTEN BY JEFF TRESSLER ON MOTHER'S DAY 1997

Epilogue

Many of the current books on spirituality offer specific exercises, affirmations and other tools to help you on your quest. This book only offers a few of those things and you have to pick them out of the text yourself (you know, things like unplugging, smiling, doodling, pollinating, hugging trees and stuff like that). If you have noticed these things and tried any of them on, then I have succeeded in capturing your attention and we have connected. If you haven't done this, but you have felt your Heart open or you have even related to the stories, well, that also means we've connected.

Perhaps the best tool that I can offer you is the poems. If one or more of them speaks to you, please copy it and use it for a guideline. Almost all of the stories in the book are contained within the poems themselves. I would be honored if you carried them with you and delighted if you shared them with others.

I also recommend listening to the songs that I have referenced as they contain golden threads of truth spun in beautiful melodies that create a frequency and a feeling that only music can give you.

At this time there is no sound track for the book, so you're on your own.

Carpe Diem!

References

OPENING QUOTE

1. Steve Winwood, "Higher Love" from the album *Back In The High Life*, FSC Music LTD, 1986

INTRODUCTION

1. Michael Franks "It's All On The Inside" from the album *Blue Pacific*, Mississippi Mud Music, 1990

CHAPTER 1

1. Caroline Myss, *Energy Anatomy* (audio cassette), Caroline Myss, 1996

2. Jackson Browne, "Running On Empty" from the album *Running On Empty*, Swallow Turn Music, 1977

3. *Nell*, Twentieth Century Fox, 1995

4. *Dead Poets Society*, Touchstone Pictures, 1989

5. *Phenomenon*, Touchstone Pictures, 1996

CHAPTER 2

1. Kenny Loggins, "Conviction Of The Heart" from the album *Leap Of Faith*, Sony Music Entertainment, 1991

2. Dan Fogelberg, "Netherlands" from the album *Netherlands*, Full Moon/Epic Records, 1977

3. Kenny Loggins "Conviction Of The Heart" from the album *Leap Of Faith*, Sony Music Entertainment, 1991

4. Allman Brothers Band,"Revival" from the album *Allman Brothers Band- A Decade Of Hits*, Polygram Records 1991

CHAPTER 3

1. Deepak Chopra, *Ageless Body, Timeless Mind,* Harmony Books, 1993

2. Michael Tomlinson, "Living Things" from the album *Living Things,* Mesa Records, 1991

3. Aldous Huxley, *Island,* Harper & Row, 1962

4. Crosby, Stills, and Nash "Wooden Ships" from the album *Crosby, Stills, and Nash,* Atlantic Records, 1969

CHAPTER 4

1. Dan Fogelberg, "Magic Every Moment" from the album *River Of Souls,* Full Moon/Epic Records, 1993

2. Dan Fogelberg, "Part Of The Plan" from the album *Souvenirs,* Full Moon/Epic Records, 1974

3. Dan Fogelberg, "Magic Every Moment" from the album *River Of Souls,* Full Moon/Epic Records, 1993

4. Dr. Suess, *Oh, The Places You'll Go,* Random House, 1990

5. Alan Cohen, *A Deep Breath Of Life,* Hay House, 1996

6. Deepak Chopra, *The Seven Spiritual Laws To Success,* Allen-Amber Publishing and New World Library, 1994

7. Jimmy Buffet, "Changes In Latitudes, Changes In Attitudes," from the album *Songs You Know By Heart,* MCA Records, 1985

8. Dan Fogelberg "Nexus" from the album *Nexus,* Full Moon/ Epic Records, 1981

CHAPTER 5

1. Alan Cohen, *A Deep Breath Of Life,* Hay House, 1996

2. Jimmy Buffet, "A Pirate Looks At Forty" from the album *Songs You Know By Heart,* MCA Records, 1985

CHAPTER 6

1. Stevie Wonder "Ebony and Ivory" from the album *A Review, A Greatest Hits Collection,* Motown Records, 1991

2. Santana"Give And Take" from the album *Borboletta,* CBS Records, 1974

3. Dr. Martin Luther King, *I Have A Dream,* Martin Luther King, 1963

CHAPTER 7

1. Dr. Naomi Remen, *The Eye Of An Eagle, The Heart Of A Lion, The Hand Of A Women,* Noetic Sciences Review, 1992

2. Eric Clapton, "Let It Grow" from the album *461 Ocean Boulevard,* Polygram Records, 1974

CHAPTER 8

1. Elton John, "Love Song" from the album *Tumbleweed Connection,* Rocket Records, 1970

CHAPTER 9

1. John Hiatt "Through Your Hands" from the album *Stolen Moments,* A & M Records, 1990

2. Deepak Chopra, *The Seven Spiritual Laws To Success,* Allen-Amber Publishing and New World Library, 1994

3. *A Course In Miracles,* Foundation For Inner Peace, 1975, 1985

4. Don Henly, "The Heart Of The Matter" from the album *The End Of The Innocence,* Cross Country/Wild Gator Music, 1989

CHAPTER 10

1. Marianne Williamson, *Illuminata, A Return To Prayer,* Berkley Publishing Group and Random House, 1994

To Order

*If you would like to order additional copies
of this book, please send $11.95
plus $4.00 shipping and handling to:
Circle of Three Publishing
P.O. Box 533902
Orlando, FL 32853-3902
OR
to order online: www.legacy-publishing.com*

*The author will personally autograph
all books at your request.*

Your comments are appreciated.

*If you would like to submit comments for
consideration for future printing in the
VIP section of the book, please write.*

Thank you,

*Jeff Tressler
jttressler@aol.com*